Transform Your World,
One Small Risk at a Time

spark

Jason Jaggard

WATERBROOK
PRESS

Spark

Published by WaterBrook Press
12265 Oracle Boulevard, Suite 200
Colorado Springs, Colorado 80921

ISBN 978-0-307-73061-9
ISBN 978-0-307-73062-6 (electronic)

Copyright © 2012 by Jason Jaggard
Illustrations © 2012 by Jason Jaggard; illustrations designed by Ruthi Auda; Spark logo design by Drew Melton

Cover design by Kristopher Orr

Library of Congress Cataloging-in-Publication Data
Jaggard, Jason.
    Spark : transform your world, one small risk at a time / Jason Jaggard.
      p. cm.
Includes bibliographical references (p.   ).
    ISBN 978-0-307-73061-9—ISBN 978-0-307-73062-6 (electronic)
  1. Self-actualization (Psychology)—Religious aspects—Christianity. 2. Change (Psychology)—Religious aspects—Christianity. I. Title.
    BV4598.2.J35 2012
    248.4—dc23

                                        2012016131

Printed in the United States of America
2012—First Edition

10 9 8 7 6 5 4 3 2 1

Special Sales
Most WaterBrook Multnomah books are available at special quantity discounts when purchased in bulk by corporations, organizations, and special-interest groups. Custom imprinting or excerpting can also be done to fit special needs. For information, please e-mail SpecialMarkets@ WaterBrookMultnomah.com or call 1-800-603-7051.

This book is dedicated to S. J.
May your life always be full of joy. I believe in you.
The best is yet to come. 🔥

Contents

Acknowledgments

To my parents, Craig and Sandy. For always believing in me.

To Mandy, Anthony, Xander, and Elijah. Who knew when we moved to Los Angeles?

To Dave, Tam, Ru, Beks, and Debs...you know what you mean to me.

To my partners in crime at Spark Good: Ryan Daugherty, Scot Burbank, Brian Roth, Jess Thomas, Mark Wittig, Tory Nelson, Alex Froehlich, Christa Scholtz, Lauren Grubaugh, Ruthi Auda, and Chuck Chessher. I absolutely love what we've created together, and it couldn't have happened without you. Here's to more heists of generosity.

To Michael Abramson, Chris McLaughlin, Johan Khalilian, and Adrian Koehler. You are forces of nature and friends for the journey.

To Jess Koehler, David and Brittany Haley, Scott Mocha, Thomas Bush, Michael Muniz, Jon Kroening, Michael Valania, and Dan Leffelaar. Thank you for spending time reading and arguing over the manuscript with me and with one another. You made this book better than it should be. You make my life better too.

To Steve Saccone. Without your help getting started, there would be no book.

To Eric Bryant. I meant what I said to you on my thirtieth birthday.

To Erwin McManus and my friends at Mosaic. Your fingerprints are all over this project. Your fingerprints are also all over me. I think that's a good thing, and I'm forever grateful for your investment in me.

Finally, to Mark Sweeney, Ron Lee, and the fine folks at WaterBrook Multnomah. Thanks for taking a risk on me and this book. Let's do it again soon.

Risky Business

/////////// ✳

For almost a decade I've been a student of why and how people change. It is said in recovery culture that people change when the pain of staying the same is greater than the pain of changing. Aside from being really insightful, that's more than a little depressing.

Of course, pain can be a great motivator of change, like when you pull your hand away from a hot stove. But thankfully, pain isn't the *only* reason people change. In fact, many times change can be...well...fun.

Think about some of the choices you've made that brought about change: going to college or getting married or pursuing an internship or traveling overseas or accepting a job offer. It's not likely that you made these or similar decisions because you were in pain.

At least I hope not.

I have friends who went to grad school not because the pain of having an undergraduate degree was so great, but because the pleasure of having a graduate degree was so much greater. Likewise, how would you react if you heard someone say, "I got married because the pain of being alone became too great"?

How romantic.

Or if someone went after his dream job and said in the interview, "I'd like to work here because the pain of working with the bozos in Department C is just too great."

Um...next.

What I love about life is that people change not only because of pain but very often because of pleasure. They change not only because their current life hurts but also because the future could feel so much better. Sometimes we change not to make something stop but to start something new. And right now, in your life and mine, there are things waiting to be made new. Right now, there is a future out there waiting for you.

And it's *good*. It's not a future of endless pain but of fulfilling pleasure. It's a future not of drudgery but of joy. And it's worth changing for. It's worth *risking* for.

You and Me and Life

The best advice I received before I started writing this book was to pick one person that I wanted to write to and write just for that person. I thought a lot about that. I thought about how I could write this book to a friend on the East Coast or a particular family member. I could pick someone of a specific spiritual background or a specific age. Faces flashed in my mind. Whom to pick? Who needs this book the most?

And after all that deliberation, I decided, at long last, to write this book to...myself. (What can I say? I'm a narcissist.)

Let me explain: I *dedicated* this book to someone else when I got done writing it. But I've discovered over the past several years that there are lots of people like me who face the same struggles I face. There are lots of people who experience the same frustrations with life as I do. I don't know anyone better than I know myself, and I wanted to write this book primarily because *I* needed it. The ideas in this book have changed my life, which is why I'm sharing them with you. My hope is that they'll be as helpful to you as they have been to me.

I Am Not Brad Pitt

Several years ago I was working with a team of college students, and they arranged it so that a group of inner-city kids could come watch a college basketball game with us. Many of these kids had never been outside their neighborhoods, let alone to a real college arena with all the lights and cheering crowds.

During the course of the game, we bought the kids pizza. As I was handing out slices, one little girl tugged on my shirt. I looked down and she looked up and said, "Are you Brad Pitt?"

White people all look the same.

At the risk of stating the obvious: I am not Brad Pitt. Brad is famous and beautiful, and he has opportunities that most of us will never fully understand. This book was not written for him.

This book isn't about how to be famous, nor is it about thrill seeking. It's not about filling the void of our lives with near-death experiences so we can say we've really lived.

This is not a book where a number of naturally likable people tell you how you, too, can become more likable. This isn't one of those books where naturally attractive and athletic people tell you how to win friends and influence people, make more money, and find awesome success. Nor will natural geniuses explain how you can raise your IQ.

I am a fairly normal guy. I have strengths and weaknesses just like everyone else. I have hopes and dreams and fears and insecurities. I'm responsible for my life, just like you're responsible for your life.

I have never gone skydiving. I have never gone shark diving. Come to think of it, I don't think I've even bobbed for apples. I don't drive a motorcycle or a fast car.

I don't search for thrills, but I do search for life. I want to live a meaningful life, and my guess is you do too.

This book isn't a typical self-help book. It's my attempt to create a road map that leads to a more meaningful life and to challenge you to take the risks required to get there. Starting with chapter 1, I'll be vigorously and joyfully *attacking* some of the most common ways we look at growth, learning, and the tools needed to accomplish both. I'll suggest that we should approach our own growth and learning in a very different, more exciting, and transformative way.

Here are some of the questions we'll explore:

- **What** does it look like to create a lifestyle of healthy risk-taking?
- **Why** do the standard ways that we learn things almost always leave us unchanged?
- **How** can we learn in different ways so we can more rapidly become who we were meant to be?

As I was writing this book, I had a list that I wrote to remind me why what I was doing was important, and it eventually found its way into this introduction. I wrote it so that when things got tough, whenever I felt like giving up, I could look at the list and be reminded that this conversation matters. It's a list of *becauses*.

The list applies to my life, to the message of this book, to my company—Spark Good—and I hope to your life as well. It serves as a manifesto of sorts for all of us who have decided that, finally, we are ready to do what it takes to change our lives and the world around us.

When the process of change takes an unexpected turn and you start to feel discouraged, I invite you to use this list of *becauses* to help you stay the course.

I do what I do *because* tonight

- **people feel** more helpless than they truly are;
- **people are** suffering from solvable problems;
- **people are** lonely and desire to know and be known;
- **people have** undeveloped potential;
- **good is** trapped underneath our fear of failure;
- **people are** busy and distracted from the things they truly care about;
- **people have** leadership abilities that are undeveloped;
- **ideas** that could change the world are trapped in our minds;
- **people are** living lives of passivity;
- **people are** bored;
- **people are** anxious and don't know why;
- **people are** restless for a deeper experience of God;
- **people are** drowning in a sea of information;
- **people are** overexposed to boring ideas that become exciting only when they are applied;

- **people's communities** have grown stale and stagnant; and
- **people have** destinies that their wills are not yet able to create.

—The Spark Good Reasons, Summer 2011

This list pretty well sums up why, in 2009, I started creating groups to facilitate healthy risk-taking so people could live more meaningful lives. We call them Spark Groups. Out of these groups have emerged beautiful stories of risk and growth.

In fact, thousands of people could tell their stories in this book. And before long, you can tell your story too. The first risk of all is one that anyone can take: just keep reading.

Creating Atomic Change

////////

Why small is the new big

Years ago I got to be part of a Q&A with Larry King, where the question was asked: "What makes a great guest for your show?"

"Four things," he replied. "They have to be articulate, funny, self-deprecating..." And the final thing: "They have to have a chip on their shoulder."

I love that. People with a chip on their shoulder are interesting. It's because they believe the world should be a certain way and it's not. And they're not afraid to say it. More than that, they think you should care just as passionately as they do about the condition of the world.

When I heard Larry's answer to the question, I thought, *What's my chip? What is it that I care about?* Since then I've thought a lot about the various chips on my shoulder.

I mean, I have so many!

That's a joke.

Kind of.

Over the years my chip has become easier to identify. When I started working with the best and brightest students at the university level, I began to notice certain trends. They were talented, smart, attractive, and generally considered good kids. Yet there was something missing.

Many brilliant students lacked fire and drive. They saw themselves as passionate, but they were passionate only in comparison to their more disengaged classmates. That's the problem when you're surrounded by people who are as bright as you are. You begin to think that being bright is normal, and you begin to live a normal life.

Many times when I was on a university campus, I felt like I was surrounded by brand-new Ferraris, able to do zero to sixty in 4.33 seconds, yet content to settle in at twenty-five miles per hour and feeling proud to be moving at all.

This angered me.

It was the one part of my story that was different from theirs. I hadn't gone to one of the best schools in the country. I didn't attend UCLA or USC or Pepperdine or Cal Tech. I'm not particularly good-looking or an especially good person. Yet when I was a junior in college, I sat down with the president of my school and pitched to him the idea of turning our school into a world-renowned center for unleashing human potential.

I hadn't thought much about that moment since it happened more than ten years ago. But as I think about it now, I realize that what I did wasn't, you know, normal.

Still, I met with the college president because I have an almost patho-logical desire to do something meaningful with my life. My friend Dave Auda once said that when he dies, his only hope is that his body will fall in the right direction so the people behind him know which way to go after he's gone. To Dave, retirement is a myth. It's even worse than a myth; it's a death sentence for committing the crime of apathy against humanity. Dave is going to give until he drops.

I know how he feels. And I want everyone I meet to feel the same way. After working with college students on a number of campuses, I real-ized what my chip was.

My chip was an empty shoulder. *Anyone's* empty shoulder.

The chip on my shoulder—the thing that inspires, frustrates, moti-vates, angers me—is that there are too many chipless shoulders in the world. Too many Ferraris with untested engines. Too many hu-mans with untapped potential.

Too many souls full of natural gas...

With.

No.

Spark.

What We Need Most

It is said that seventy-five percent of Americans are chronically dehy-drated. And it's interesting that one of the symptoms of chronic dehy-dration is that you're not thirsty.

Think about that for a second: when you're desperately in need of water, you have no desire for water. Take right now, for instance. Are you thirsty *right now*?

As I write this, I wouldn't say that I'm thirsty. But now that I think about it, I haven't had a glass of water since around eight o'clock last night. My muscles are tight. I feel a little fatigued. My lips are dry. My body is in need of water and yet I don't *feel* thirsty.

Sometimes the things we need most are the things we think we need least. When I was a resident assistant in college, they taught us how to work with students who were depressed. The big secret to helping these students was to get them out of their rooms. Get them up and moving. Get them out among people.

But when you suggest that to a depressed person, she will almost always say she doesn't *want* to. When you're depressed, the *last* thing you want to do is be around people.

Yet it's the best thing for you. The thing you need most is the thing you want least.

Which brings us to the tension we experience when we consider taking a risk. When we started creating Spark Groups all over Los Angeles, we called them "risk groups." Over and over we noticed that people were nervous about participating. When we asked why they weren't interested, they would tell us that *risk* is a scary word. Sadly, these were the people most in need of taking some healthy risks.

That's the thing about risk: it might be exactly what you need, even though you don't sense a need for it. Taking healthy risks is necessary for all of us, but it's also one of the easiest things to set aside. It's something we think we'll get around to later when there's a more convenient time.

We all need conversations and groups and spaces in our lives to help champion our fragile desire to take the risks we were meant to take. It's not easy to find these spaces because life offers so much resistance. Generally, we encounter four obstacles to the idea of our taking a risk:

1. It's scary.
2. It's lonely.
3. It's negative.
4. It's dangerous.

Let's take a look at each obstacle. First, it's scary. I have to agree with this one. Taking a risk is stepping into the unknown. It's uncomfortable. And while these things are true, risk is also fun, so when we launched Spark Groups, we decided to make the experiences fun.

Second, risk can be lonely. This obstacle is easy to understand. We usually keep our riskiest behavior to ourselves. That way if we fail, no one will know about it. So with Spark Groups, we decided to put risk where it belongs: in the context of community.

Third, risk is widely viewed as a negative thing. Just thinking about risk can cause people to break out in a cold sweat. A common view is that risk involves putting your head in a lion's mouth. And even when we think of risk outside the context of a circus, there are plenty of negative terms that come to mind: *at-risk youth* who engage in *at-risk behaviors* that will, generally, ruin their lives. So with Spark Groups, we encourage only positive risks or what we call healthy risks. A healthy risk is anything that makes you a better person or the world a better place.

Finally, risk is usually thought of as dangerous. That's an obstacle for a lot of us, and when this objection is raised, we respond, "You got *that* right. Welcome to a more interesting life!"

Overcoming the four common obstacles to risk is the essence of Spark Groups. Spark Groups are social experiences that have been field-tested in more than ten countries and engaged in by more than ten thousand people. Participants have come together at colleges, in corporations, in churches, in youth groups, in inner-city after-school programs, and even at a homeless shelter.

Because the longing for change is universal, there are no limits on who can start a Spark Group or who can participate. It begins with a small group of people who agree to encourage and support one another in an experiment in risk. They further agree to meet together for five weeks as each person takes four risks (one per week) that are guided by this single question: "What's one risk I can take this week to make myself a better person or the world a better place?"

That's when sparks begin to fly.

What Is a Spark?

So what *is* a Spark? A Spark is a choice. A small risk. It's a flash of light that brightens the everyday routine of your life. It's a decision to move from inaction to action.

Oftentimes we can look at our lives—our work, relationships, hobbies, and even our spirituality—and wonder if we'll ever arrive at where we want to be. Will we ever be as productive as we want? Will we ever be the friend, spouse, parent, son, daughter, boss, or employee that we long to be? Will we love greatly? Will we unleash our full potential? Will we have the impact on our world that we dream of?

These questions can seem daunting, even unrealistic. Our dreams can inspire us, but they also can haunt us. When we were younger, our dreams took us to the stars; they inspired us and drew us into the future. Yet as we got older our dreams began to grow dim. Now we have to pay the rent and get the oil changed and buy new outfits and keep in touch with friends and show up at work. It's not long before we can no longer see the stars: they get lost in the glare of our every-day lives. Yet the stars remain, waiting to be rediscovered. If only we'd take a look.

The reality is we don't know how far we can go in life. We don't know how much good we can create. We can't know for sure which stars in the night sky belong to us. Our destiny, in many ways, always remains a mystery.

And yet...while we can't be sure about how far we can go, we do know this: we're meant to go further than where we are today. We can't deny the urge inside us to be different and to make a difference. We might not be able to reach the sky, but we can step into the opportunities that are right in front of us. We can take risks. We can do the one thing that no one can do for us: take responsibility for our lives and our own progress.

At any given moment progress is only one risk away. We're always one healthy choice away from changing the trajectory of our lives. We don't know our destinies for the next five or ten years, but we know what's available to us right now, and what we can do next. At any moment we can choose to do something that is different from what we've tried or avoided before.

And just so no one is misled about this, it always involves taking a small risk. Few four-letter words are as threatening as this one. You go out there and take a risk; who knows what might happen? It could blow up in your face. You could make the biggest mistake of your life.

I hear the same cautionary voices you do, and they are the voices that keep us from changing our lives and bringing about change in the world. Many of us prefer driving to flying because if we run out of gas in a car, we can steer it over to the shoulder. Whereas a plane without fuel is headed in only one direction, down. But risk is the stuff of life, the necessary next step, the energy that keeps us alert and alive and trying things. Sure, we never know the end from the beginning, but if we did we'd be bored out of our minds.

Still, the word *risk* can be a little scary. That's the tension: risks are scary but necessary; they're uncomfortable but required to live a meaningful life. To manage this tension we'll focus on small risks. *Spark* isn't necessarily about making radical changes. Often, the best thing to do is something small that will turn into something big later on. And some risks aren't even all that risky when you stop to think about it. They are simply the right thing to do. You do it because not to do it would be wrong. And later on, you realize how big a step it really was.

I have heard the stories of hundreds, if not thousands, of people who have participated in Spark Groups. Again and again I hear a similar tale: risks that seem small are the ones that can change you forever.

The Power of Atomic Risks

One of my favorite stories to come out of the Spark movement has to do with a big dream and a young woman named Lauren. The first time I met her, she struck me as a quiet person. But she has a subtle power that makes her able to lead. When Lauren joined a Spark Group, she started by taking this risk: to tell a coach at her school that someday she wanted to work with Olympic athletes.

Looking at it from the outside, it doesn't seem like this would be the scariest conversation to have. Okay, coaches can be intimidating, and Lauren's dream was a little like saying, "Hey, Coach, I want to be more successful than you are." Sure, there's that. But she seemed determined to raise the issue, and with this particular coach. So the rest of us were eager to hear how it went.

The next week Lauren came back to the group and told us what happened. She had gone into the coach's office and immediately felt nervous just being there. *What if there's nothing he can do?* she wondered. Eventually she was able to spit out why she came to talk. She didn't mean it to, but it came out like a confession: "I want to be an Olympic trainer someday."

There was silence.

The coach took a deep breath and then said, "Lauren, to even have a chance you'd have to do an internship in Colorado Springs at the US Olympic Training Center."

"And that's really hard to do."

Lauren's spirit sank. She looked down at her hands just as the coach was picking up a phone. He dialed a number and she heard him say, "Hey, Margie! It's been a long time. How's Colorado? Yeah. Hey, listen, I've got this girl here who needs to come out and do an internship with you this summer."

He handed the receiver to Lauren.

The next thing she knew, she was at the Olympic Training Center in Colorado Springs, networking with some of the most gifted trainers in the world.

Small risk. Atomic results.

When I first heard Lauren's story, a thought struck me: What could happen in my life, and in your life, if we each chose to take just a little more risk? Not a huge risk, but one that is doable. What if you chose to take a risk this week? What might happen?

What I love about Lauren's risk is how nondramatic it really was. I mean, all she did was have a conversation. If we had peeked into the office during her meeting, we would have seen a coach behind his desk and a young woman sitting in a chair. There were no fireworks, no sweeping musical score. Just a short conversation, a phone call, and a changed life. The risk was small; the change that followed was huge.

And that's exactly the point. Life change sneaks up on us. To an outsider it looks like a conversation. But to Lauren it was the start of a new life.

A Movie of Your Life

Life, most of the time, isn't all that dramatic for any of us. Right now I'm typing away at a computer, wearing pajamas and sporting a head of hair that's going everywhere. Later I'll grab lunch with my sister, do some consulting with a high school in Pasadena, volunteer with an after-school program in downtown Los Angeles, then come home and write some more.

It's a good life; I enjoy what I do. But it's just life. And I'm going to guess that your life is also not all that exciting on an everyday basis.

But here is the truth that we often miss: that's where all the *good stuff* is.

I'm all for making life more interesting. That's one thing our company, Spark Good, is all about. In fact, sometimes when I'm traveling and people ask me what I do, I say, "I work with a company that creates an experience to make your life more interesting." It's a great way to begin a fun conversation.

Taking a risk will always make your life more interesting. And you'll find, afterward, that taking a risk, by definition, will change your life in some way. But most of the choices you make are not "film worthy." In other words, the results usually do not warrant a dramatic musical score that swells behind the high suspense. Yet somehow, as you take small risks, it creates a life that *is* worthy. You can add to your highlight reel by choosing to change, and small risks are what get you there.

Over the past few years, as the Spark movement has spread across the country and into other countries, people have reconnected with estranged parents. People have changed careers and started non-profits. People have changed the way they treat their bodies or their families or their finances or their world.

These make for great stories, and I love to hear them and tell them. But really, most sparks are smaller than that. Most are simply choices to make the week a little less ordinary and a little more beautiful. Sending flowers to a loved one. Going for a job interview and really doing what it takes to make an impression. Taking time to volunteer for a cause. Giving away some money. Extending friendship to someone who previously had escaped your notice.

You have to start somewhere, and starting always involves risk.

The great tragedy of our lives isn't going to be that we took small risks instead of big ones. The great tragedy will be that we took no risks at all. Risks are like exercise—a flexing of the will. When you start an exercise program, the immediate result is sore muscles, stiffness, blisters, and discomfort. You don't experience sudden weight loss or dramatic gains in strength. You have to trust that taking the risk to exercise will result, eventually, in an improved life, better health, and greater well-being.

When you trust that the first step will lead to something good but as yet unseen, you are flexing your ability to let go of outcomes. You are now trusting something greater than yourself. You take a risk, follow through with where it leads, and then start looking for the goodness that it produces. In every instance it involves getting outside your comfort zone to choose something beautiful and out of the ordinary.

At least that's how it started for me.

The First Spark

A few years ago I spoke on "finding your passion" at a leadership con-ference at Pepperdine University. I was wrapping things up when a thought hit me: I could take a small risk by trying out my ideas about finding your passion—just to see what might happen—or I could sim-ply end my talk. I didn't have time to think it through, and I knew it could flop. But something about it just felt right...so I went for it.

"Here's the thing," I said to the audience. "I don't know a ton about discovering *your* passion, but I do know that you don't discover your passion by listening to someone talk about it. You discover your pas-sion by taking risks, by getting outside your comfort zone and seeing what sticks and what doesn't.

"So," I continued, "for the next few weeks I'll drive here to Malibu and we'll find a time and a place to meet. Every week, each of us will take one risk to either make ourselves better people or the world a better place."

There wasn't any magic. No fireworks. Around ten students signed up. But ten was enough for a good experiment, and the following week I hopped in my car to see what would happen. As I drove up the coast, I started getting texts from students saying they weren't going to make it. Nobody ever calls to reject you. They just text you. Or send an e-mail.

This bummed me out, but hey, when you take a risk, you take a risk. I knew there was no guarantee that the experiment would work.

As I walked up the stairs to our meeting place, I heard what sounded like a party. Just perfect, I thought. It's going to be me and three other students trying to make ourselves heard over the noise of a great party taking place across the hall.

Then I walked into the room, and what I saw shocked me. The space was *packed* with students. We didn't have ten show up—we had twenty! Word had spread and people wanted to join in the experiment.

For the next several weeks we had a blast. We didn't really know what we were doing; none of us had tried a thing like this before. But we knew we were on to something.

And Spark Groups were born.

You don't know where a risk will lead, but you go ahead and take the risk and see what happens next. In my case, a company happened next.

Spark Good exists to create cultures that value the role of risk in personal development and to resource groups of people who have decided to band together and take small risks for positive change. I am passionate about helping people cultivate an appetite for healthy risk-taking. It's my conviction that through the act of taking healthy risks you will discover your passion, your thirst for life, and the chip that sits on your shoulder, and that you will become the kind of person you were meant to be.

That's why I wrote this book.

So if you're ready, all you need to do is answer and act on one question: What is one risk I can take this week that either makes me a better person or the world a better place?

Let's get started.

The Spark of Life

//////////

*When the dust settles,
what we're truly after*

Elizabeth Gilbert, author of the wildly successful book *Eat, Pray, Love*, spoke at the TED conference in 2009.[1] She recounted the artistic history of communities in North Africa from several centuries ago. Part of their tradition was to hold beautiful tribal dances that would continue through the night, ending the following morning. Occasionally, something wonderful would happen.

In Elizabeth Gilbert's words:

> Every once in a while, very rarely, something would happen, and one of these performers would actually become transcendent. And I know you know what I'm talking about, because I know you've all seen, at some point in your life, a performance like this. It was like time would stop, and the dancer would sort of step through some kind of portal and he wasn't doing anything different than he had ever done, 1,000 nights before, but everything would align. And all of a sudden, he would no longer appear to be merely human. He would be lit from within, and lit from below and all lit up on fire with divinity.[2]

On fire with divinity.

Not only have many of us witnessed this type of phenomenon, perhaps during a virtuoso performance or a film or sporting event, but some of us have also *embodied* this sort of thing. It is that moment when time slows and life becomes more full, more tangible, more beautiful. Like we're lit up from within. Maybe it's been on a stage or at work or on a field. We've experienced glimpses of something magical. Something extraordinary.

When this would happen in North Africa, Gilbert explains, something strange would occur: "People knew it for what it was...they called it by its name. They would put their hands together and they would start to chant, 'Allah, Allah, Allah'..."[3]

In other words, "God, God, God." They were catching a glimpse of God.

> When the Moors invaded southern Spain, they took this custom with them and the pronunciation changed over the centuries from "Allah, Allah, Allah," to "Olé, olé, olé," which you still hear in bullfights and in flamenco dances. In Spain, when a performer has done something impossible and magic [the audience shouts], "Allah, olé, olé, Allah, magnificent, bravo," incomprehensible, there it is—a glimpse of God.[4]

Gilbert was speaking primarily about the arts. She was encouraging artists and artisans to give themselves to their craft, even if divine inspiration never strikes again (or even a first time).

Yet it would be a shame to limit her message to a career or craft. There have been moments for me, aside from any speech I've given, aside from any book I've written or film I've produced, when I sensed the presence of the Divine—when I felt lit up from within. Not in my career but in my character. Not in my work but in my relationships. There have been moments full of love, strength, and compassion.

There have been brief moments when I felt that I was filled with something that can be described only as Life.

Dare I say that I was on fire with divinity? It was a glimpse of Life, a glimpse of God.

In my most vulnerable, most honest moments, Life is exactly what I long for.

Life is a near-constant theme throughout the Christian scriptures. In fact, one of my favorite passages outlines the evidences of Life. These are also the evidences of our connection with God. The spiritual activist Paul of Tarsus listed these evidences of Life to the ancient city of Galatia in the first century.

He wrote about love.
He wrote about joy.
He wrote about goodness
               kindness,
                    gentleness,
                         patience,
                              and self-control.[5]

It's far from an exhaustive list, but it's a beautiful characterization of the life that I truly long for. The kind of life we all long for.

I want a life full of rich, rewarding love. I believe we all do. We all long for lives that are profoundly, deeply, unexplainably joyful. And while we may not always be aware of it, we have a deep longing to be truly

good, to be honorable and compassionate, to be able to look ourselves in the mirror and admire who we see. We crave kindness. We
admire those who are strong yet gentle, patient, and in control of their
thoughts, attitudes, and actions.[6]

That's the kind of person I want to be. And the scriptures whisper,
"That is Life. That is where God wants to lead you."

The scriptures record Jesus as saying, "I came so that humanity
could experience full, rewarding, vibrant Life."[7]

Being fully alive is not about your level of education or how wealthy
you are. Being fully alive is not about the kind of car you drive, the size
of your house or bank account. It's not about how many awards you've
won or whether people appreciate what you do. It's not about your
sense of style or whether you got a promotion and a bonus this year
or how good-looking you are. We may want some of those things, and
we may eventually obtain many of them, but they're not—in and of
themselves—Life.

Life is available to you and me and everyone else—no matter how
accomplished you are, or how admired and loved, or how overlooked you might be. Life is available at any moment, and at every
moment.

It simply has to be chosen.

The Life You Want Versus *Life*

There is a difference between the life you want and Life. The life you
want takes into account your goals, dreams, and ambitions. You may

want to be married someday. You may want to have kids or grandkids. You may want to retire from your current career and invest your remaining years in a different pursuit. You may want to obtain a certain job or earn a promotion or graduate college or get a master's degree or a doctorate. You may want to win a championship or play a musical instrument or perform on a Broadway stage.

The life you dream about is out there at a distance, while the things that appear immediately in front of you are challenges and obstacles. None of this is bad. We all need dreams and goals that pull us into the future. But the life we want is not the same as Life.

Yet sometimes it seems like Life is too hard to find. Like it's hiding from us. Life is a glimpse of God, but why does it seem to be beyond our grasp?

The Life That Is Right in Front of You

I am notorious for losing things. Keys, sunglasses, socks, books, pens, my car. I've probably spent more time wandering around in the Disneyland parking lot than I have at Disneyland.

The most embarrassing times are when I'm looking for my keys and they're in my pocket, or when I'm looking for my glasses and I'm wearing them. After years of trial and error, I've learned that if I can't find my glasses, the first place to look is on my face.

Sometimes the things we're looking for are right in front of us.

That's the difference between the life we want and Life. The life we want is in the future, but Life is always happening, all around us, all the time. The life we want can seem far away, yet at any moment... even at this moment right now...Life is available to all of us.

A promotion? In the future.

Peace? It's available right now.

Life isn't so much about achievement as it is about access. It's not so much about possessions as is it about passion. It's not so much about living standards as your loving standards.

What would it be like if you got a sense for Life and realized it's available to you every second? What would your life look like if in every conversation, every choice, you could have beautiful, vibrant, passionate, terrifying *Life*?

If this is possible, what would it take for you move from the distant life of your dreams to the Life that is available right now, waiting to be discovered?

From Lazy to Living

I have a friend named Dave. The best way to describe him is to picture a white Will Smith, and then make him the most laid-back dude you've ever met. He's funny, a natural athlete, smooth.

Through high school and college, though, he struggled to find his niche. If you asked him today about his college experience, he might say that those years were largely wasted. He grew up in a privileged part of town, attended an excellent school, and often was bored. I think he'd say that back then, he was more than a little lazy. This was the Dave that I knew in high school.

Fast-forward seven years later when Dave found himself teaching junior high students in the inner city. The school he works at is called a KIPP school. KIPP stands for "Knowledge Is Power Program." These charter schools, which started in Los Angeles, are some of the premier systems of education for children born into poverty. The founders of the KIPP methodology authored the *New York Times* bestseller *Work Hard. Be Nice.: How Two Inspired Teachers Created the Most Promising Schools in America.* Dave's school was featured in the award-winning documentary *Waiting for "Superman."* His school has been studied by some of the world's brightest minds in the field of education.

These students—because of reasons beyond their control—are some of the hardest kids to teach. They eat teachers for breakfast, so why would someone like Dave—a self-proclaimed lazy, entitled young man—go there to teach?

Here's the only reason I can think of: Dave today is not the Dave I knew in high school. In fact, when Dave is in the classroom, he becomes something else entirely.

Watching Dave teach inner-city students is like watching a symphony conductor with a background in improvisational jazz. In any given thirty seconds, he praises a student, sternly warns another, empathizes with them both, says something funny, teaches something important, asks a question, praises an answer, and sternly warns another student.

Rinse and repeat.

It's exhausting just to watch him. The range of emotional flexibility and leadership he commands in thirty seconds is more than I experience in a week. Yet he makes it look effortless. In fact, he enjoys it. When Dave teaches, he offers onlookers a glimpse of Life. A glimpse of God.

When I see him do his thing, I can't help but say "Olé!" Put Dave in a classroom and he's fully alive. He becomes wise, compassionate, competent, encouraging, a source of Life for his students. He's so good at what he does that Meg Whitman, the former CEO of eBay, came to visit his classroom to see what was going on.

This from a kid who did essentially nothing for four years in college.

What happened?

Well, after college, instead of getting a cushy job making six figures and living the rest of his life on easy street (which is where he was born), Dave decided to take a huge risk and participate in an experience called "Mission Year."[8]

Mission Year is a one-year experiment in which you maintain the standard of living of the poorest Americans—for twelve months. You live where they live; you attend church and shop where they attend church and shop; you live on the salaries they live on. You don't have the latest mobile device.

And that one choice, that one risk, changed the path of Dave's life. It was risking that created the context for his life to unfold in a profound and beautiful way. Taking a risk didn't just help him achieve his goals. It didn't necessarily make him more successful in the eyes of anyone who was watching. It was not even linked to a big dream that he had, at least not in any intentional way. But taking one risk helped him become the kind of person he had been longing to be. It pointed him in the direction of Life.

How to Tap into Life

There's a saying that one hundred percent of what you want out of life is outside your comfort zone. You can see the truth of that when you consider your biggest dreams for the future. If you're going to launch a business, you'll need start-up capital and partners with the right areas of expertise. You'll have to develop a realistic business plan and the right contacts, line up vendors, recruit a sales force, and create a brilliant marketing plan. No one has to tell you that getting ahead in life—making it big—requires risk.

But what about laying hold of Life, one that is full of goodness and joy and love and patience? That requires the greatest risks of all.

We want a life of peace, but choosing peace is a risk. We want to forgive others and to be forgiven, but choosing forgiveness is a risk. Choosing love, goodness, and kindness; choosing to practice self-control. These are Life's greatest risks.

They also are where Life is found. And believe it or not, God is calling us to something even *greater*.

A Well Becomes Her

The scriptures tell about a woman who had devastated her life through a series of broken relationships. In her search for love, she encountered one-night stands, affairs, and broken promises. In her desperate search for intimacy, she ended up alone. She was so hurt and jaded from broken relationships that she would go to the village well at the hottest time of the day just so she wouldn't be subjected to the prying eyes of other villagers.

On one especially hot day, she was at the well, hoping no one would see her. Unfortunately, a man who was sitting near the well asked her to draw Him some water. They made small talk for a while, and then the conversation took an unexpected turn. The man said He had water that was far better than what this lonely woman had been drinking. It was an odd statement, considering that the man had just asked the woman for a drink of water.

The woman was a realist, and she called attention to the obvious. If the man had this great water, why was He asking her for a drink? He looked at her and said, "Everyone who drinks from this well will be thirsty again. But whoever drinks of the water I give them will not only never thirst again, but will become a well with water springing up from within them."[9]

The man she was talking to was Jesus, and He wasn't talking about water.

He was talking about Life.

To be fully alive is not simply to drink deeply of life and to be satisfied. It's to become a well, offering Life to the world around you. That is what it means to be fully alive. It is not only to experience a glimpse of God for yourself but also to become a glimpse of God and to create communities that are glimpses of God.

Communities of "Olé!"

It is my belief that you were designed to be an extraordinary human being and to live your life in the context of extraordinary community. Your destiny doesn't necessarily involve fame or fortune. But I promise that it does involve the greatness that comes from making beautiful choices alongside others who are striving for the same thing.

So how do you and I get there? Well, it is unleashed through risk. When the dust settles, it's what we truly want. It's what we truly need.

But until we lay hold of it we are but giants, sleeping.

THREE

We Are Sleeping Giants

///////////

I stand among giants, sleeping.
Adventure and defiance, safe keeping.
Good goes undone
Between battles not won,
While the world suffers violence, weeping.[1]

Napoleon is said to have declared China a sleeping giant. He then said, "Let her sleep, for when she wakes she will shake the world."

What if his words were true of you and me? What if we are giants, but asleep to the world?

I know what I'd say to Napoleon. I'd say, "Well, I don't feel like a sleeping giant. For starters, I'm not asleep. I'm talking to you right now. Also, I'm not a giant. I mean, sure, I'm tall. But not *giant* tall."

Case closed. Now let's talk about the weather.

But what if I was wrong? Just to make sure, let's start by talking about sleeping.

The Dangers of Sleep

Sleep, that mistress of the night. When I was younger I was drawn to her like a siren. In my college and post-college years, there was nothing I looked forward to more than sinking into the blankets and wrapping both arms around a pillow and drifting away. Didn't matter if I'd worked hard that day or if I had wasted the day in mindless diversions. In fact, for some reason, having wasted the day usually made sleep better.

I could sleep all day. When I was in college, on Saturdays sometimes I would try.

I was an addict, really.

Looking back I think I liked sleep because it was an escape, a way of shutting down so I didn't have to deal with life. All destructive behavior is a form of escapism. It's a form of sleepwalking.

Pornography is an escape from intimacy. Gluttony is an escape from health. Laziness is an escape from success. Bitterness is an escape from forgiveness.

We want Life more desperately than anything else, yet we run from the beautiful things of Life. Life is attractive, but also terrifying because of what it demands of us. To drink deeply of Life requires us to be humble, courageous, generous. It demands the best from us and more.

It demands the Divine.

And so we sleep. In our more honest moments, we can admit that we're sleeping in one way or another. And when we're awake, neutral things and even good things can become distractions—sleeping pills for the soul.

Entertainment.

Work.

Technology.

Relationships.

It's one thing when people and activities enhance our lives. It's another thing when they sedate us.

Why We Need Jerks

We're all familiar with the weird jolt that we sometimes get right as we're falling asleep. Our eyes are closed. We begin to feel safe and relaxed. Our heart rates and breathing slow down. We're embarking on that nice, slow drift into dreamland, the place of rest and peace.

And then, right before we fall asleep...

BAM!

It feels like we're falling, with nothing to grab on to and nothing to catch us, and our bodies almost literally rock us awake.

I hate that feeling.

What's occurring in that moment is that our brains sense our breathing rates and heart rates slowing down and interpret that to mean we are actually dying. The brain isn't super excited about dying, so it triggers a pulse of adrenaline to wake us up.

It's called a myoclonic jerk. (I learned that from watching *House.* I love that guy.)

When you think about it, we all need jerks. We need moments that wake us up from our reliance on escaping from the world, from our propensity to become apathetic.

I'll tell you about the jerk that turned my life around. It happened several years ago, at a time when my life was moving in all the right directions. I had a great job, a huge office, a big budget. I had more money than I could have imagined just a few years earlier. I even had an administrative assistant and a girlfriend. (They were not the same person.)

I was working with a large nonprofit that was involved with high school and junior high youth. We had experienced a pretty good year. The programs I was in charge of had doubled the number of youth participating. We had multiplied our leadership six times over.

And my life was falling apart.

I had no idea what I was doing or why, and even less of an idea how to fix it. We had a huge event coming up that would attract a thousand students. It would feature a stage production that I had insanely thought I could write (on my own). And we were behind schedule. (The truth is, I hadn't written anything.)

Then, right before the holidays, my girlfriend told me we were over. It was the same day I'd gone out to buy the engagement ring.

My life fell apart. I learned later that Twelve-Step programs talk about a moment of clarity. It's the moment when you see your life for what it really is. It's a waking-hours myoclonic jerk. It lets you know that your soul is dying. It's a pulse from God to wake you up.

It can take just about any form. You get fired, you lose someone close to you, or you work hard to achieve a goal and find that it isn't at all what you really wanted. These moments shock your soul into looking around and within—taking the time to ask the hard questions.

It's a moment of spiritual sobriety. You'd been sleeping and didn't know it.

The jerk that wakes you up could involve just a part of your life. Maybe your life as a whole is not asleep, but a significant portion has dozed off. Perhaps it's a relationship, your career, or your interior world. Maybe it's in the impact you are making or not making in the world. Maybe it's your finances or health or your spirituality.

There is a nagging sense that you are, in some fashion, asleep, and life is passing you by.

You're a giant, and it's time to wake up.

The Whisper Within

When I was in high school, every summer a group of students and adults would travel to inner-city Dallas to run a camp for local kids. We would take a bus with no air conditioner down Interstate 35, from Kansas City to Dallas, through hundreds of miles of territory with temperatures exceeding 100 degrees. To get some relief from the heat, we'd bring along the biggest cooler we could find, fill it with ice, and take turns sitting in it. The high school students bonded as we suffered the heat, sweating through our shirts and shorts, waiting for our turn in the cooler.

It was some of the most fun I'd ever had. Those trips were extremely formative, allowing me to spend extra time with adults I respected and to get involved in doing something meaningful.

One of the things I looked forward to the most was going on morning walks with my mentor, Darren, the guy who organized the Dallas trips. He was a kind man, one of the most sincere leaders I've ever met. During one of our walks, he asked what I was learning on the trip. And as we walked back to the rooms where the group was staying, I was struck with this...sense. I recognized a deep desire within, and I wanted to share it with Darren. So I took a deep breath and sputtered, "I think I'm supposed to do something great with my life."

As soon as the words were floating in the air, I felt like an idiot for having said them. It's not the kind of thing you normally hear in casual conversation at the office:

Richard: "Hey, Larry, how are things?"

Larry: "Oh good, good. Just reflecting on my sense that I'm meant to do something great with my life."

Richard (silence): "Well, good luck with that."

We may not talk about it in office cubicles or at parties, but it is something we all sense at some point. It just feels weird to admit this nagging sense that we each have a destiny. It sounds grandiose. It sounds arrogant. Who do we think we are, anyway?

Exactly.

We are giants.

Back to the Entrepreneurs

Jesus didn't indicate that this type of thinking was grandiose or arrogant. Quite the opposite. One of His favorite stories to tell was the story about a wealthy Venture Capitalist who gave money to three entrepreneurs, and then went on a long trip.[2] Person 1 got five talents. Person 2 got two talents. And person 3 got one talent. We'll explore this story more fully later, but for now, what strikes me is how much money a talent is. When I was a kid and heard this story, I pictured a "talent" as a small coin. So I assumed Entrepreneur Number 1 got five coins, Entrepreneur Number 2 got two coins, and Entrepreneur Number 3 got one.

I pictured the last guy holding one pathetic little coin. I imagined him taking his coin out into the woods and then digging a hole with his hands. I'd see him placing the coin in the earth as if it were an acorn, covering it, and then patting down the dirt on top so no one would discover it.

No harm done.

Even now when I hear the story of the entrepreneurs, I encounter a nagging thought. Pretty much, I'd love to be the five-talent guy. Maybe some of you are thinking you're the two-talent person—not too rich but not too poor. Sometimes I wonder if I'm the one-talent guy. It can be a convenient excuse.

"Don't expect too much from me," I say. "I've only got one talent."

So you can imagine my shock when I realized that just one talent equaled the accumulated earnings of a person who had worked at minimum wage for twenty years. If the three entrepreneurs were alive today and were being entrusted with money to invest for the top guy, the *smallest* amount of principal would be almost a half-million dollars.

Entrepreneur Number 2 got a little more than $1 million. And Entrepreneur Number 1 was handed $2.5 million.

A couple of thoughts:

First, it gives you a whole different picture of Entrepreneur Number 3 digging a hole to bury his one talent in the woods, doesn't it? If I had to bury cash like that, I'd have to rent a backhoe or at the very least hire a couple of guys to help me dig a hole big enough to hold a half million.

Second, Jesus shows us that even the person who received the least had a small fortune to invest for his master. I mean, I sure wouldn't mind someone investing 500k in my business.

The point is clear: maybe you and I have more talent than we think. Not necessarily singing or dancing or doing both at the same time (please, no). But we have huge potential. Maybe we are most deeply asleep when we minimize all that we have to offer.

When Your List Is Too Small

I work regularly with college students, and in workshops (and sometimes in class) I ask them: "If you could create the ideal life, what would it look like?" The answers vary, but generally the list looks like this:

Own a home.

Travel.

Raise a family.

Have a job that I enjoy.

Get married.

Have fun.

I then ask the students to rank, on a scale of one to ten (ten being the hardest), how difficult they think it will be to accomplish the six frequently mentioned goals. I usually hear eights and nines. The truth is that, statistically, nearly everyone in the room will accomplish most of the items listed. And if you're an adult, you've probably accomplished at least half of them already, or have intentionally not achieved these goals for other goals that mattered more to you. Good for you.

None of the things on the list is bad. We all share a desire to be with people who love us, to enjoy meaningful work, to have enough money to pay the bills, and so on. It's not easy to do these things, but neither does it require superhuman effort or intelligence.

Let's admit it: we have set the bar too low.

We've listed the obvious things, the things most people are satisfied with. But we need to take a close look at what is *not* on the list.

Billy Graham, the great spiritual leader of the twentieth century, had all the items on that list. But that's not all. He and his friends led a spiritual movement that impacted millions. Dr. Martin Luther King Jr. had all the items on that list...and he and his friends led a movement to promote justice and equality in the United States.

For three years I taught a class at Pepperdine University called "Power and the Human Spirit." We explored what it meant for each of us to be made in the image of God, and how that starting point shapes our role in the world. We took a close look at how each person's uniqueness and ability to partner with God qualifies that person to serve humanity.

For one class assignment, my students had to write a short story about their own funerals, as though family and friends would be honoring the most extraordinary life anyone had ever lived. The emerging generation has been accused of idealism, laziness, arrogance, and a sense of entitlement. I admit that I expected the stories to venture into fantasy.

What I got was far less than that.

My students wrote stories about being decent wives and mothers, husbands and fathers. Of living a simple life, even keeping mostly to themselves. It seemed the list of the six basic goals in life, including landing a job, marrying well, having a home, and raising children, was still alive and well.

Again, there is nothing wrong with these goals. But what about living for more than that? What about the poetry of life that lifts it above ordinary? What is lacking from our aspirations, causing us to fall short of what philanthropist Bob Goff calls "strategic whimsy"?[3]

The stories written by my students, and the lists that my workshop attendees tend to come up with, reveal how little we expect from ourselves. The reality is that we are made in the image of God. We are full of potential. Even if we have just one talent, it means we're sitting on an incredible pile of cash.

A desire for greatness has been embedded into our spiritual DNA. Some of us deny that desire and settle for far too little. Other times we'll do anything we can to make our mark in the world.

Even if it's the wrong mark to be making.

FOUR

Our Power Is Not
the Problem
//////////

The ancient story of Us[1] as told in the scriptures recounts a strange scene. Sin had entered the narrative, and humanity was experiencing sin's consequences. It was a time of great pain but also great ingenuity. Not all our beauty had been tarnished.

Humans were beginning to invent music and tools and architecture. And as the story goes, our ancestors got an idea to build something extraordinary—something that never had been seen before.

A tower.

Forget Trump. Forget Eiffel. This baby was going to be legendary. A beautiful tower stretching into the sky, a declaration of the genius and power of humanity. And that makes sense, if you think about it. We've been making stuff to show off our power ever since.

What is odd is God's reaction to the construction project. He saw what humanity was doing and got nervous. "We have to stop this," He said.

Now, I hear that and I think, *C'mon, God, don't be such a downer. What harm can a tower do? Just let people do their thing.*

And God's reasoning doesn't really help me much. God says: "For if they do this, then nothing will be impossible for them."[2] So God scattered the people and gave them different languages so it would be hard for them to understand one another—harder for them to collaborate and work together.

And if you're like me, you're thinking, *That's not very nice. He's a big God, and He sees us playing in the sandbox down here, having a good time with our tower, and what does God do but kick over our tower and then make it hard for us to work together.* It makes God look like some kind of transcendent bully.

Again, God explained His actions, saying if He didn't intervene, nothing would be impossible for humanity. But I'm thinking (and maybe you are too), *Why would that be a bad thing?*

Then I started to think about it more carefully. I thought about when I'm ticked at my friend over some imagined slight. Or when I'm driving on the I-405 freeway and someone cuts me off. Or when people chew with their mouths open.

In those moments I have this overwhelming desire to retaliate.

To Show the World My Power!

When some guy in an expensive sports car cuts me off in traffic, it's good that a lot of things are not possible for me. Reality keeps me from retaliating.

And that's just me and the small slights I endure. Think about gangs in any major American city. I'm glad that for MS-13, the most dangerous gang in the United States, some things are *not* possible.

Then I think about corrupt politicians. I think about dictators. I think about Nazi Germany.

Then this thought hits me: maybe God's decision to slow us down wasn't an act of bullying but an act of compassion. It stopped us from hurting ourselves even more than we already had. It wasn't our power He was worried about. It was our character. If anything, the ancient story about God's intervention is an *affirmation* of our power.

We are giants.

But we also are wounded and broken giants. Our power is intact, yet our character has been shattered.

It's easy for us to get things backward: we think too highly of our character and too little of our power. We think we're pretty good folks, for the most part. Not too good and not too bad.

But powerful?

Eh.

Yet poet Marianne Williamson wrote: "Our deepest fear is not that we are inadequate. Our deepest fear is that we are powerful beyond measure."[3]

Frankly, I'm afraid of both.

On Being a Giant

Most homes I've visited have staple features: Living rooms with couches and televisions. Kitchens with microwaves and refrigerators. And most homes have the most sacred space in all the land: the snack drawer.

I love me some snacks! Twinkies. Swiss Rolls. Essentially anything that didn't have to die before it was processed and packaged and delivered to a grocery store. If it's loaded with artificial sweeteners, it gets preferential treatment.

My parents used to buy these totally soft, completely unnatural cookies with about two inches of thick synthetic frosting on top. The cookies came in a clear container so you knew when there was just one cookie left. Or worse, no cookies left.

One night when my parents were going out, my dad did a quick run to the snack drawer to pick up a cookie for the road.

Yet there was none.

My dad's posture stiffened. He was not a violent man, but he loved him some snacks too. He turned to my mom and said, "Someone ate the last cookie."

Now here's my beef with what happened next. Do you think my parents even asked my sister if she ate the last cookie?

Nope.

Both my parents looked at me. Me! I was just sitting there, doing my homework.

"Jason," they said, "did you eat the last cookie?"

I told them meekly I was innocent. INNOCENT!

They didn't believe me.

There was no evidence, mind you. Only speculation, abetted perhaps by a touch of intuition.

One of my least favorite feelings is being falsely accused. Or when someone looks at you like they know what you're thinking when they don't. Drives me crazy. So I got all worked up and began to make my defense when suddenly my parents realized they were late to wherever it was they were going.

"We'll talk about this later," they said. And then they were gone.

I had not even been given a chance to explain myself. I was livid!

I found myself in the computer room. (For those of you who grew up with laptops, a computer room is the room where the Apple II with a blue screen was housed—right next to the dot-matrix printer.)

I was pacing. And talking to myself. Out loud.

"I can't believe they think I ate the cookie! I didn't eat the cookie! This is wrong. This is injustice!"

Then I looked at the wall facing me and a thought popped into my head: *I bet I can punch a hole in that wall.*

I, like my father, was not prone to violence. I don't think I had ever hit anything. Yet before I could convince myself that this was an altogether stupid idea, I had shouted like Jackie Chan and thrown my clenched fist at the wall as hard as I could.

I had a lot of time to think while my fist flew through the air. I thought about the wall. About the hidden but real two-by-fours holding up the Sheetrock. I remember thinking, *This could be very bad.* So I closed my eyes in the hopes that it would somehow make it better.

There was a moment of silence.

When I finally opened my eyes, my arm was fully extended. My fist had disappeared through a hole in the Sheetrock.

I had punched a hole in the wall.

In that moment I had two overwhelming thoughts. The first was, *I just punched a hole in the wall. My parents are going to kill me.* The second sounded like this: *I just punched a hole in the wall.*

I. Am. *Awesome.*

I strutted from the computer room to my bedroom. I was the *man.*

Sure, I soon became a grounded man (two weeks, I think). But to show you my parents' sense of humor, they hung a sign over the hole that read "When life gives you lemons, make lemonade." It stayed there for years.

Thinking back on this, I try to understand why I punched a hole in a wall. It was and remains to this day a stupid thing to do. It had something to do with feeling weak when I was falsely accused of eating the last synthetic cookie. I felt misunderstood, but I wanted to feel strong, empowered.

Even if that meant doing something bad.

I wanted to make an impact, even if that impact was destructive.

I think this essentially describes the human condition. We stay pretty busy trying to make our mark on the world, to alert the universe to our presence and significance. And sometimes we turn to destructive choices simply because they seem to be the most readily available and provide the fastest form of relief. It's better, we may tell ourselves, than feeling weak and helpless.

Sometimes it's not necessarily that we're bad. It's that we're bored, so we channel our boredom into destructive choices because the beautiful choices are either not apparent to us or seem unattractive. It's not necessarily that we don't want to be constructive; it's that our imaginations have atrophied. We no longer see the beautiful possibilities in front of us or within us.

Blind to all that is available to us, we start to believe there are no options, and our power—our leadership—goes wasted.

On Impact

One of the most terrifying statements I hear is when parents claim they are not leaders. I think they mean they're not necessarily going to run a company or run for public office. That they're not always the smartest or most competent person in the room.

But I have a hard time separating *parenting* from *leadership.* If you're a dad, you're a leader. If you're a mom, you're a leader. Honestly, if you're a son or daughter, you're a leader. If you live in a neighborhood or apartment complex, you're a leader. If you're a boss or an employee, you're a leader. Leadership is impact, and everyone impacts those around him or her in some way.

Part of being human is wrestling with the reality of your impact on the world and stepping into the challenge of intentionally making your impact one of beauty and love.

My favorite definition of the word *character* is "a defining mark." Think of the twenty-six letters in the English alphabet. Each letter is different and has its own character and distinctiveness.[4]

When I was a child, I learned how to type on a typewriter. For you kiddos, a typewriter was this heavy piece of machinery where you pushed a key (like a computer keyboard) that caused a little hammer to slam a piece of metal into an inked ribbon, which impacted the ink in the shape of a letter onto a sheet of paper. You knew what key you had pushed from the mark that the metal made on the page. Sometimes, even if there wasn't ink left in the typewriter ribbon, you could still see the dent that pushing the key made in the paper.

You could still see its impact.

For a typewriter, character and impact are inseparable. We are really no different: our character is defined by the impact we make in the world.

It's interesting that there is no word for "character" in ancient Hebrew. You'd think this would be a problem when trying to describe the character of God. How do we describe something without a word for it?

Interestingly, the word *kâbôd* in Hebrew is the closest to the English word *character*. *Kâbôd* conveys the idea of weight or impression or heaviness. Impact.

But the way we translate this word is "glory." What this means is that the glory of God is inseparable from the impact and character of God.

This is good news to me because sometimes when the scriptures speak about God being all about His own glory, it can come off as a little, well, narcissistic. We don't particularly enjoy people who are all into themselves. It makes God come off like some diva rock star, asking for bottled water chilled to a certain temperature and with the cap loosened. Yet I hear people say, "Well, He's God—He can be that way."

I suppose.

But couldn't God's glory mean something entirely different? When the ancient scriptures speak of God being first and foremost about His glory, I think it means that God is, first and foremost, about His own impact. Could it be that God is not primarily about fame and recognition, but rather the essence and substance of His impact on the universe? And that His impact flows from His character?

I suppose this could be a little narcissistic as well. It kind of depends on what type of impact God wants to have.

To gain a better understanding of God's glory and His impact on the universe, it helps to look at the character of Jesus. When we do that, we see a dominant theme emerge. Paul of Tarsus wrote that Jesus was God, and that because He was God He became a servant. Jesus taught that all who desire to be extraordinary human beings must serve others. Jesus said about Himself that He came not to be served but to serve.[5]

The One in the scriptures who is said to have shown us who God is, spent most of His time engaged in acts of compassion and mercy. By doing these things, He was essentially saying, "This is what God is like."

So what we learn about the glory of God, and about His impact, is that He is a servant. When we see that God's impact—His character—is one of servanthood, we begin to gain understanding. God says He is about His own glory, which means He is about serving and loving all of creation—everything in existence.

And then God does the unthinkable: He invites us into the same adventure.

That's why every Spark Group wrestles with the question: "What's one risk I can take this week to make the world a better place?" It's the same as asking, "What's one way I can serve others?" Another way to put it: "How can we reflect the character and impact of God?"

How can we create as many moments of "Olé!" as possible?

Serving the Future You

There is a second question that members of every Spark Group ask: "What's one risk I can take this week to make myself a better person?" For some folks this may seem self-serving, but it's not. You are an investment that needs to be stewarded wisely. Mastering self-investment and self-leadership is one of the most powerful ways you can serve the world and those around you.

Put another way: it's one of the best risks you can take.

A few years ago a friend was going through a really hard time. He was busy but not feeling fulfilled. He was surrounded by people but didn't feel known by anyone. He had been engaging in some fairly destructive habits. It's a common place to be, and it's a really dangerous place to be.

My friend is a young, uber-talented, superlikable guy. He creates a lot of positive energy when others are around him. When he moves, people follow him.

But one night when we got together, he wasn't doing too well.

Sometimes the pressure gets too intense or the loneliness goes too deep, and we start making decisions that go against who we were meant to be. My friend and I were sitting at a table at a café at LAX. His shoulders were slumped in fatigue. The flame in his soul barely flickering. He was a powerful human being with so much to offer the world, but he was battered and wondering what to do next.

Just like you and me.

I could see my friend's character, even though he was having trouble seeing himself clearly. "Tonight," I told him, "your actions affect only a small number of people. Your friends, your family, some of the people you lead. But that's now. Tomorrow things will change, and now turns into tomorrow quicker than you think."

He looked over at me, and I couldn't help but think, *I love this guy so much.* (Hey, Bromance is a recognized film genre, so why not?)

And then, before I could stop talking, these words came out:

> You are destined to lead. It's in you and I know it's kind of a crappy deal sometimes, but that's the way life goes. So although it seems your life is small right now, your influence is going to get bigger. Probably a lot bigger. Which means the mistakes you make are going to get bigger too. Which is why we're having this conversation now and not later.
>
> These issues in your life—it's time to start working through them. The "you" twenty years from now needs the "you" today to start working on things *right now.* You don't want to be twenty years older and still be wrestling with these same choices. The twenty-years-older "you" will have way bigger problems, way greater challenges to deal with. You'll have a wife and kids, and responsibilities that would scare you to death if you knew about them right now.
>
> So for the sake of the future "you" and the thousands of people you will be leading, fight this. I believe in you. I know God wants to help you step into your future. I know you want that too. So do it, and know that you've got a friend for the journey.

We finished our coffee (actually, I got orange juice because I hate coffee), paid the waitress, and went our separate ways. I drove home with the Los Angeles cityscape reflecting off my beat-up car, wondering if I'd said too much or if I hadn't said enough. It's hard to know sometimes.

I had attempted to give him a myoclonic jerk, hoping to wake him up. I didn't want his soul to die. I knew he was destined to lead others, but he had to choose for himself to pursue Life. He had to take the risk to fight against the ever-growing current that was pushing him downstream, trying to prevent him from becoming extraordinary.

From Jerks to Sparks

We can ask these hard questions all night long. But things don't begin to change until we move from asking hard questions to making hard choices. In fact, sometimes asking the hard questions can be a distraction from making the choices—and taking the risks—we're called to make.

There's a difference between a myoclonic jerk—being suddenly put on alert—and a spark—your response to that alert to do something different from what you've done before. A jerk happens to you. A spark is something you make happen. A jerk wakes you up; a spark moves you forward.

Jerks are God's gift to us. Sparks are our gifts to the world.

We've all been there. Can't you relate to my friend's potential, his sense of destiny? Can you relate to his tendency to keep drifting, and can you sense the danger that he might choose not to fight the war in his soul that is necessary if he is to become a person full of integrity and power?

Can you hear again that fragile whisper that you rarely talk about, which says you were meant for something extraordinary? You might have been wrestling with these things for a long time. It may already be late, but it's never too late. You and I simply have to unlearn a few things.

FIVE

Learning Ourselves
to Death

/////////

*Redefining what it means
to learn something*

For many years I worked with a nonprofit called Awaken, which conducted daylong workshops to help people unleash their natural talents and develop unnaturally deep character. We used, among other tools, an assessment called the StrengthsFinder, developed by the Gallup Organization and Donald Clifton, a leading researcher of human talent.

To develop the StrengthsFinder, the Gallup Organization spent more than twenty years interviewing over two million people who were the best at what they did. The best doctors, lawyers, teachers, athletes, and janitors—you name it. They spent time figuring out what it was that made those people great at what they did. Out of that mountain of research came an assessment that helps people identify their neurological sweet spots for productivity and satisfaction in work and life. It is an amazing assessment.[1]

The information presented during the Awaken workshops is life changing. Over the course of five years, our team coached and taught several thousand people. We worked with colleges, businesses, think tanks, and churches. Remember, we were using one of the best performance assessments in the world. And the folks I worked with were some of the most gifted and talented presenters and leaders I'd ever met.

Yet we kept noticing the same pattern. Attendees would take the assessments and process the information, but their lives wouldn't change. We would meet people weeks, months, or years later and find that they couldn't remember what the results of the assessment were, let alone how the results should have shaped how they manage their time and energy.

And this is even more unexpected: most participants didn't seem concerned about the disconnect. They felt that they had benefited from attending the workshop even without any long-term effect on their lives. You see, the workshop was highly entertaining (we put a lot of energy into making it so). The presenters were fun, and the coaches were personable. Just being there for a day and bathing in such powerful ideas was a great experience for people. But it didn't necessarily change them or help them change themselves.

So people who went through the training consistently asked the same question when it was over: *Now what do I do?*

The attendees had all the information they needed. What they lacked was the will and the skill to apply the information. The content had made it to their minds. But it had not, as of yet, made it to their feet. Instead, the information lay buried, like woolly mammoths trapped in permafrost.

What Did They Learn?

If you asked people what they had learned at an Awaken event, they might say, "We learned about our talents and how to leverage them in our lives." But if you followed up by asking what they were going to do differently the following week, they'd be hard pressed to come up with an answer.

And therein lies the problem: sometimes we say we've learned something just because we've heard it and can repeat it back to you. I might be able to articulate every leadership theory known to humanity but still be a horrible leader. I can recount the main points from a marriage seminar and still be a below-average spouse.

You and I have not learned something until we can put it into practice. The most important knowledge in the world—knowledge about relationships and ethics (or how we treat one another)—is most powerfully expressed in action rather than in concept.

It doesn't really matter what you "know" if learning stops with knowledge. As the ancient saying goes, "Wisdom is proved by her *deeds*."[2]

It is said that knowledge is power, but you have to apply it first. You haven't learned it until you can live it.

This is a hard truth to embrace because, at first, it really diminishes what we think we know. It causes us to question ourselves. *Have I learned joy? Have I learned patience? Have I learned love? Have I learned how to make the most of my one and only life?*

These can be uncomfortable questions to answer. They are revealing questions if we choose to answer them, but they are also easy-to-ignore questions. We have to fight the urge to grade on a curve, to compare ourselves to others. We have to avoid rounding up to the next highest score. Rounding up won't make us into the people we long to be, and grading on a curve won't help a hurting world.

The hard reality is that a book, conference, or workshop won't get us to the place where we are doing the things necessary to change our lives and to change the world around us. We can't read our way into more joy or listen our way into helping others. We have to choose. It will require that we change, not just agree with some ideas.

Yet there are forces working against us, often in the form of lessons we learned years earlier that we now need to unlearn.

Learned Helplessness

I recently heard a haunting story about the research by psychologist Martin Seligman. He described an experiment involving a dog that was put in an empty room. The dog ran into the room, excited, eager, and happy—as most dogs are. Then the researchers passed an electric current through the floor.

The dog yelped and jumped, trying not to touch the floor. It continued to jump and yelp until finally—worn out and numb from pain—it gave in to the reality that the shocks were never going to stop. So the dog lay down, simply giving in to the electric shock.

What happened next is even sadder. The researchers put the same dog in a different room. An electric current ran through the floor, but this room had an exit. A door stood open, offering a way to escape the suffering. But even with a nearby escape available, the dog lay down on the floor, giving in to the shock. The dog had given up on the possibility that a solution to its problem could be found.

Seligman calls this phenomenon "learned helplessness." It refers to past experiences in life when we were taught that we're helpless when in reality we're not.[3]

One of the most misunderstood and misused concepts we are exposed to is the idea of helplessness. Of course, there are things we are powerless to change. Part of emotional sobriety is being able to admit our limits. Yet too often we think we're helpless when we're really not.

Falsely believing we are helpless makes the human will impotent. It is the most dangerous kind of myth. In ancient times, myths were told and retold to give meaning to life. But the myth of helplessness does the opposite, draining meaning from life. It says that we have no choice, that the way things are today is the way things will always be. In our relationships, in our work, and in our world. In our lives.

We at Spark Good invest our efforts in combating this life-denying myth. We call learned helplessness "suffering from solvable problems."

Every morning we wake up to face challenges, obstacles, and hazards. These problems seem insurmountable, and that's what trips us up. What seems impossible to get beyond, in almost every case, is solvable. Things can change. We can change. But we never will change as long as we believe we can't. To overcome learned helplessness, we have to move to learned empowerment. It's the shift from living a reactive life to a responsible life.

The One Thing Necessary for Growth

A few years ago a study evaluated more than five thousand nonprofit organizations that exist to help people develop into better human beings. The study found that much of the work done to help people grow not only failed in that mission but actually got in the way of people's growth. Much of what was done to "help" others actually *hurt* them.

The study concluded that one prerequisite for personal growth super-sedes all others. There is one trait in the human spirit that unlocks more opportunity than any other: personal responsibility. People can't grow unless they are willing to take personal responsibility for their lives.[4]

It is true that some things are outside our control, and in those in-stances we must reach out for help—an act that is its own form of personal responsibility. However, there is a great gap between what we *think* we're capable of and what we're *actually* capable of.

While it may be your manager's job to help you grow in your work skills, the bottom line is that you won't grow unless you're willing to take responsibility for your own growth. While it may be your parents' job to raise you, at a certain stage of maturity your parents can't help you any longer. You have to want to grow.

So how do we learn to take personal responsibility? Where are the spaces, the classrooms, the environments and communities that help us assume responsibility for our lives?

Spaces for a Change

Los Angeles is home to some of the most famous comedy clubs in the world. The Groundlings Theatre, the Laugh Factory, the Ice House, iO West—just to name a few. The Ice House in Pasadena is the oldest comedy club in the country, and the Groundlings Theatre is where many *Saturday Night Live* alumni got their big breaks.

If I were to ask ten different people why they go to a comedy club, nearly every one of them would give the same answer. They go to a comedy club to laugh. Laughing is a gift, and a great comedian is totally worth a two-drink minimum and twenty bucks for the cover charge.

You judge comedians by only one standard: whether they make you laugh. Now people might not agree on whether a certain comic is funny, but that doesn't stop people who go to comedy clubs from expecting that night's comedian to *be* funny.

Imagine how strange it would be if we expected something different from comedians. Something random. For example, imagine hearing someone say, after watching Jerry Seinfeld, "Man, I didn't enjoy that at all. I still don't know how to change my oil."

Yeah, I guess if that's what you were expecting, you'd be disappointed. He wasn't up there to teach you auto maintenance. He was there to make you laugh.

"I didn't get anything practical out of that speech Conan O'Brien just gave."

Okay, that wasn't a speech. It was a monologue.

"Why was he telling all those jokes?"

He's a comedian.

"Where's the whiteboard and overhead projector?"

Not a classroom.

What we expect from an environment will shape how we assess the environment and what we get out of being there. We go to comedy clubs to laugh. We go to movies to be entertained. We go to sports stadiums to watch our teams win.

Most of us understand that the goal is to have a good time.

But what about other environments? What about, say, therapy? Or an Alcoholics Anonymous meeting? It would be a little sick if people said they go to therapy for entertainment.

We should expect the appropriate things from the appropriate environments based on the purpose of those environments. For example, the purpose of A.A. is a specific kind of life change. The same could be said of therapy. We go to therapy when our lives aren't working well and we need someone to help us sort through the mess. Again, the purpose is life change.

There is a huge difference between A.A. and a sporting event. The latter is a place you go to cheer; the former is a place you go to change.

Now we need spaces to cheer. We need spaces to help us laugh. And just as important we need spaces that help us change.

To grow.

To become.

We all need spaces in our lives where the goal is life change. Yet sadly, there are very few environments that are designed to facilitate life change. And often the ones that do exist have massive PR problems.

Take churches, for example. For some of you, *church* is an offensive word. It conjures old feelings of old buildings and old people singing old songs and listening to a boring sermon. It often is a space where people go to pretend to be good without all the fuss of having to actually be good. If that's your perception, I totally get it. Just bear with me.

If you stood outside a church on Sunday morning and asked those leaving the service whether they liked it, you'd hear some "nos," a few "kind ofs," and a few "yeses." But if you asked them *why* they did or didn't like it, most would say one of two things:

They'd mention the sermon.

They'd mention the music.

Either they liked the sermon (it was funny, insightful, inspiring, they agreed with it); or they didn't like the sermon (it was boring, arrogant, uninformed, they disagreed with it). Either they liked the music (it was beautiful, they liked the style, the musicians were talented); or they didn't (the music was dated, the musicians lacked talent, the songs were poorly chosen).

Very rarely would you hear an answer that addressed how attending church had helped or hindered personal life change. It's not often that you would hear a person say, "I loved the message because now I can go home and [fill in the blank with a beautiful choice they wouldn't have chosen if they hadn't been at church]." You almost never hear "I love coming here because this is the best place for me to become the person I want to be."

Not many of us go to church thinking it will help us change, because most of us don't expect that from a church. We might expect our kids to be taken care of, hope to see people we know, look forward to meeting new people. We might expect to hear something new from the Bible and to sing meaningful songs. Maybe we go to be entertained and possibly inspired.

But change our lives? "Whoa buddy, calm down," we might say. "I'm just here because I like being here." And that's the problem.

This is the question that has been stuck in my mind for years: where are the spaces we regularly put ourselves in so we can change and grow? Without them our lives fall into ruts. Without those spaces we never truly unleash our potential. Without those spaces our lives aren't as rich or rewarding as they could and should be.

So where are the spaces for change?

Those of us who launched Spark Good set out to identify those spaces and to make them widely available. We wanted to create spaces that embodied three elements:

- **They needed to be risk oriented.** (This is in contrast to most small-group experiences, which focus more on information and teaching.) We wanted people to show up expecting to take a risk that week and for that to be the focus of the group.
- **It needed to be social** (versus therapy, which usually is one-on-one). We believe life change happens best and most authentically in the context of community. I love therapy, yet often it can devolve into paid friendship or a place where people share what they want to share to increase the chances of hearing what they want to hear.

- **It needed to be accessible** (versus Twelve-Step programs, which usually are issue specific and can be very intense and intimidating). I have benefited from the Twelve-Step movement, yet sometimes the intensity of the problems people share can scare others away. We wanted our spaces to be fun and meaningful.

How to Lead a Spark Group

Here is how it works. You and several friends or acquaintances, from ten to fifteen people, agree to get together once a week for five weeks. That part is easy, assuming you all can agree on a meeting time. Who doesn't look forward to meeting with like-minded people every week? It's a change of pace, a welcome break in your schedule.

The next part is simple: during your time together, have every person choose one risk each week that will either make him or her a better person or the world a better place. The risk can involve a change to your own life, or it can be something you'll do to make the world around you better. It could be in any area of your life where you want to step outside your comfort zone and do something you wouldn't ordinarily do—maybe your career or relationships or spirituality. And you take this risk either to invest in yourself or in someone else.

It's not easy to decide to take a risk and then to follow through. That's why it's essential that you do this with a few other people who are committed to doing the same thing. In the group each person shares what risk he or she is going to take. During that week everyone goes out and takes action to improve their lives or to improve the world.

Everybody in your group is taking a risk, every week. You reconvene once a week to compare notes. You tell your stories. Some will be funny, others will be heartwarming, and a few will be disappointing.

And that's okay.

You will discover that taking a risk to change your life, or your world, changes things. It's nothing like reading about it, staying up late to theorize about it, or talking with a friend about the what-ifs. This is a rubber-meets-the-road, real-life, going-out-there-and-trying-things experience. We both know that not everything will turn out the way you want it to, but many of the things you try will far exceed your expectations.

Where You Are the Content

Sometimes people ask us about Spark Groups, "Where is all the content?" They expect to be following a detailed study guide and wonder why we don't have one. To them, Spark Groups sound so simple. Too simple. Ten to fifteen people, for five weeks, taking four risks, and answering just one question?

That's it?

Admittedly, the steps and procedures for our groups are sparse. We do have a leader's guide and a participant's guide along with a few other resources, but we've kept them as minimal as possible.

Thus the question: Why so light on content?

The answer: Because *you* are the content.

The content of Spark Groups isn't found in a study or a small-group resource. The content is provided by the *people who participate.* Their dreams, fears, problems, hopes. Their risks. Their lives.

Look, if we pulled together a mountain of quotes, stories, illustrations, video content, and ancient wisdom and gave it to you in a guidebook, you'd have a landslide of information. And we *could* provide that, because we have access to more information than any of us wants to hear about. But we chose not to do that, because content-heavy material becomes just one more distraction. It lures people into information mode rather than application mode. You don't need more content; you need to choose. The most important conversation that takes place with Spark Groups is your life and the lives of those in the group. We ask, "What does each one of you plan to do to grow as a human being or to make the world more humane?"

Spark Groups are not a library where you go to read. They're not a theater where you go to be entertained. Spark Groups are a gym where you go to work out your will.

They're not spaces where you have conversations about risk. They're spaces that actually facilitate your taking risks.

You can spend years talking about risk, but your life won't change until you start taking risks. It's not enough to know the information. It's not enough to have the conversation. You have to move to application.

Spark Groups are one of the few spaces available to you where application *is* the conversation.

Good-Will Fitness

When I was a student, our university got a brand-new workout facility. The architecture was state of the art. The building was several stories high. It was clean and sleek. The perfect place to get your sweat on.

What's fun about new workout facilities is that everyone goes to check them out. It's very populist that way. Even people (like me) who should never go to the gym went to the gym. Granted, I didn't hop on the front-row treadmills where the beautiful people go to show off. I went up to the third floor, the poorly lit area of the new facility. But at least I was there.

So this one time I was working on the machines (free weights scare me) in my little corner of the gym, and after a few minutes I noticed a guy off to the side who was staring at me.

I tried not to stare back and just kept doing my thing. But about ten minutes later I noticed the guy was still staring at me.

So I untangled myself from the machine, walked over to the gentleman, and asked, "Can I help you?"

He looked at me and, in a thick Slavic accent, said, "You have a very unique body."

"Yeah," I said. "That's why I'm here. To change that."

Turns out, the guy was a professional trainer. He informed me that I was using the machines wrong and that if I continued to do it, I would hurt myself.

Ah. Thank you very much, kind sir.

When it comes to our lives, we often do the same thing: we tend to use the machines wrong.

Our will—the most sacred part of who we are—cannot be trained by information. It can be trained only by the choices we make. Who you are at your core is most powerfully impacted not by reading these words, but by making different choices after you read these words. Information can be a catalyst for change, but the spark is created once you actually make a change.

You can go to a thousand classes on managing your money. You can learn all the tricks, all the theories. But until you start *choosing* to manage your money differently, you haven't truly learned a thing. You can get a PhD in social justice, but until you start applying that information in direct action to bring about justice, it's just theories, facts, and stories stuck in your head.

Knowledge has its place. And it does its best work when it moves you to make choices.

SIX

From Ruts to Risks

//////////

Breaking out of routine to create something new

I love learning.

I could read all day, every day. I was one of those obnoxious students in college who could have continued taking classes forever. You know, a kid who didn't pay attention in class and then crammed the night before and got As.

I collected books as if it were my job. Looking for a book on string theory? You can read mine. Maybe a book on sixteenth-century maritime war strategy? No problem. Spirituality? Pick a religion. Leadership? Well, which function of leadership? Vision, team building, execution, creativity? My shelves are packed with books.

I have friends who own plenty of books they have never read. Amateurs, I say. *Poseurs*.

I've digested more than ninety percent of the information that's lined up on my bookshelves. It used to be like a personal discipline. Buy a book, read a book, keep a book. It was a rhythm that felt good. And frankly, I just liked having the books around—they were my intellectual trophies. Some people hunt big game and put the heads on a wall. I read books and put their used carcasses on a shelf.

I felt so empowered. So learned!

For years, getting my hands on more information was my go-to for any problem. If I was struggling in life, I knew the solution was out there—I just hadn't discovered it yet. There had to be some website or conference or idea that had the information I needed. And if I could just get there, I'd find my answer and all my problems would be solved.

That approach works great in theory, but we live in the real world.

A few years ago when I took another look at my shelves of books—and noticed books on leadership, relationships, spiritual health, and a lot more—this thought struck me: *If I had simply applied one idea from each of these books, my life would look drastically different. No, it would look drastically* better.

I'd always loved learning, but I didn't seem to love growing. My whole life I thought I needed more information, but that had not led to a drastically better life. Now I was beginning to realize that what leads to a better life has less to do with information and more to do with different *choices.*

We're all tempted to give too much credit to information. Never in the history of the world has so much information been so readily available. So our problem is not that we don't have access to information. Our problem is our inability to leverage that information to the betterment of our world and ourselves.

We keep learning, but we keep missing the reality that we possess the God-given capability to translate what we know into how we live. Nine times out of ten, we know the right thing to do, but we lack the will to carry it out. If we know so much, why are we so unlikely to change?

One word gives us the answer: ruts.

Ruts That Rock

For the first forty-one days after conception (yahoo!) your brain has no neurons. It is, really for the only time in your life, a blank slate (sorry, Aristotle). Then, suddenly, all that changes. Around day forty-one you get your very...first...neuron.

• ← there it is. (Exciting, isn't it?)

Just three months later you'll have a hundred billion of those. This means your developing brain will pump out ninety-five hundred neurons every second for ninety days.

Oh, but we're not finished. Two months before you're born, all hundred billion of your brain's neurons decide to reach out and make a connection...namely with other neurons. It's kind of like neural speed dating. Except they're serial speed daters. Over the next three years, each of the billions of neurons makes fifteen thousand connections. Each connection forms a neural synapse, the basic brain makeup. This means that by the time you're three years old, your brain has 1.5 quadrillion neural synapses. It's the most complicated your brain will ever be. (This explains why three-year-olds are such a joy to be around.)

Sadly, by the time you graduate high school, half of the synapses are gone.

What remains is the essential physical framework for what the Gallup Organization calls your "naturally recurring patterns of thought, feeling, or behavior." It's the physical side to who you are.[1]

These pathways define our talents. They are powerful forces that we can harness to make ourselves more productive in our relationships and in what we do, either at work or on our own time. When we operate inside our talents, life is easier, more fulfilling, and more energizing.

This is an example of how ruts work to our advantage. Essentially, talents are the ruts in your brain. They're ruts, but they're positive ruts. They are ruts that can be leveraged.

Living in a rut can help you become more efficient. Ruts help you outsource some of your cognitive functioning so that you can pay better attention to more important things. It's like pulling into your driveway twenty-seven minutes after leaving work and then having the terrifying realization that you can't recall driving home. How did you make the evening commute without plowing into a garbage truck? Simple. Your body just knew what to do.

Ruts allow you to get maximum output from minimum input. It's a kind of neurological muscle memory. You can do so many good things without even thinking, and it makes your life so much easier.

Yet ruts, for all their time-saving benefits and increased efficiency, can become obstacles. This is because ruts are naturally resistant to change. And when it comes to better relationships, a more fulfilling life, or serving humanity, change is the starting point. You can't improve your life or make the world a better place without change.

Ruts of the Imagination

The most dangerous ruts are ruts of the imagination. You look at the world and see the same thing every time, because ruts are like blinders on a horse. We see only what we've always seen. This makes seeing new possibilities nearly impossible. It keeps us getting what we've always gotten out of life, for better or worse.

Many years ago when I was working with inner-city youth, instead of creating programming for them, I decided to ask what kind of programming they'd like. The question came as a total shock to them. *What would they like?* Most of the students didn't say anything, and I felt defeated before I'd really gotten started.

Then one student spoke up with an idea. And then another. Soon the students were ecstatically building on one another's ideas. I furiously took notes as they explained what would be the perfect programming.

It was what they wanted.

It came out of their still-developing souls.

It was empowerment at its finest. It was brilliant. Glorious.

And it was an exact replica of what we were already doing.

I looked at the list and pointed this out to them. They blinked in amazement. How could they have created a new program that duplicated our old program so exactly?

I suggested we try coming up with something different, since what we were already doing wasn't working.

"We got nothing," they said.

Lest we be too hard on them, I've done the same exercise with students in high school and college, as well as with adults, in a variety of settings. What emerges is surprisingly consistent: half-baked ideas or exactly what we've done before.

All from the question, What do you want? It's even worse when dealing with what people need.

We are bombarded by a nonstop slideshow of images and messages tweaking and twitching our frazzled emotions. So when we're asked "What do you need?" it's a little like watching a lotto ball roll out of the churning basket. When something pops out, that's the thing we notice. And since it came to mind, it seems like it's worth mentioning. What all this says is that we are trying to identify our wants and needs in a way that is disconnected from our deepest sense of self.

Life is racing by, and we're just trying to keep up with the basics. When asked an important question, it's all we can do to catch our breath, give a quick answer, and race off to rejoin the program already in progress.

And that's a big problem. When the reference point for our current choices is the same thing we've chosen in the past, we remain trapped in what we've always done. That's a rut that prevents us from growing.

Ruts can take the form of behavior, but the most powerful ruts are ones of perspective. There's a saying: "Change the way you see, and you'll change the way you behave." But the converse is also true: changing our actions plays an integral role in shaping the way we think. There's a dance that takes place between our perspective and our behaviors. Action and thinking affect each other, and that mutually reinforcing loop shapes our being.

What's beautiful is when people begin breaking out of their old ruts of imagination and begin to dream new dreams of things that never were. George Bernard Shaw wrote: "You see things; and you say 'Why?' But I dream things that never were; and I say 'Why not?'"[2]

That's what a spark is. It's a risk of "why not?"

One Woman Awakes to Help Others Sleep

A few years ago a woman named Jennifer read Erwin McManus's book *Wide Awake,* which inspired her to begin searching for opportunities to make a difference. And that same year the Academy Award–winning film *The Blind Side* came out. It had an impact on Jennifer that she wasn't expecting. The film tells the story of NFL star Michael Oher and his relationship with a family that took him into their home at a pivotal time in his life. In one scene his guardian mother, Leigh Anne Tuohy, shows him his new room, which contains a bed.

"It's nice, I never had one before," he says.

"What, a room to yourself?" Leigh Anne asks.

"A bed," he replies.[3]

That scene inspired Jennifer with a great idea: to create a nonprofit dedicated to providing beds for the homeless and raising awareness of the crisis of homelessness. Yet that idea remained buried for months until she joined a Spark Group in Santa Monica, California.

"I joined a Spark Group mainly with the intention of meeting new people," Jennifer said. "Little did I know that it would be the first step in creating a vision worthy of my life."

During the five weeks of the Spark Group, she took a risk each week to lay the foundation for creating a company. Two years later her company, A Good Night Sleep, has given away more than five hundred beds to the homeless.

Jennifer read a book that helped her start thinking differently. Then she saw a movie and thought, *Why not?* Her normal routines as a wealth manager in Los Angeles didn't lend themselves to her starting a nonprofit company. But why not give it a try? Why not devote time and energy, meet new people, and engage more fully in the narrative of kindness and beauty that God is crafting in the world?

She took a risk of the imagination to step outside of her ruts and the everyday routines to create something new.

"There are a lot of good ideas in the world," Jennifer told me. "Being a part of a Spark Group created a platform for me to realize my dream one risk at a time. As we all know, it's one thing to ponder an idea, and it's quite another to take action to bring it to life."

What I love about Jennifer's story is that she wasn't content to just be inspired. She didn't just learn about the homeless crisis in America. She wasn't just aware; she became engaged.

That is the key to living a sparked life: capturing inspiration and translating it into action.

So what inspires you? What film or story or issue has touched you in the last year? What would it look like for you to take the first risk, as Jennifer did, to begin doing something about it? Maybe it's volunteering. Maybe it's having a conversation with a friend or spouse about the next steps to take. Maybe you have some discretionary resources or access to resources that could help move this along.

Whatever it is, do it. Step out of the ruts of everyday life and step into the unknown. Learn more about the issue or need, but don't learn just for the sake of learning. Learn for the sake of living the kind of life you were meant to live.

SEVEN

When Good Goes Bad

///////////

The perils of suburban spirituality

Not long ago *Forbes* magazine declared the county where I grew up as one of the best places in America to raise a family.

I know. Hot dang.

When I lived there, we called our city Candy Land. There was very little crime, poverty, or illiteracy. There was very little genuine drama in our clean homes and not much happening on the fiercely manicured lawns. So we did what normal human beings do when they lack a healthy sense of drama: we created a wonderful universe of melodrama. We got excited about high school football rivalries, we pimped out cars, we competed in popularity games, and we got worked up over all sorts of inconsequential issues. We were a segment of comfortable society that was going mad with boredom.

Right out of college I spent a few years working with high school students in the city where I grew up. When I talked about my job, I referred to it as "working with troubled youth." You might be picturing urban kids drawn into gang violence or kids on drugs, generally pursuing a life of crime. Yet those weren't the kids I worked with, for the most part. These kids mostly came from intact families. They got good grades. Very few of them were involved with illicit drugs or antisocial behavior. In general, they did surprisingly little of anything.

And that was the problem. In my mind they were troubled not because of the bad they chose to do, but because of the good they didn't choose to do.

One girl, however, was different. She opted not to choose good, but she at least chose something. Her name was Kate. She was seventeen and was smart and funny and had a sense of her own self. She was totally disrespectful of authority, and she was obviously one of my favorites.

While she had a sense of her own self, that sense often would lead her into what is thought of as typical, destructive teenage behavior. Every now and then that lifestyle would hurt, and she'd find herself in my office, crying and confused and looking for help.

One time she stopped by to talk about all the pain she was going through. After I listened for a while, I brought up God.

God. Two consonants and one vowel that hit Kate like two punches to the stomach and a slap across her tear-stained face. It was almost like a physical assault. Her eyes grew wide, and she launched into an emphatic explanation of why God was definitely not what she was looking for.

I will never forget her words: "I can't give my life to God. If I do that, He'll make me a nun."

Ah yes. Of course. He'll make you a...

Wait a second.

At first her reasoning surprised me. But after I thought about it, I realized it made perfect sense. She had the same view of God that I had when I was growing up. Namely, that following God is boring.

Years earlier, I had thought of God as sort of a cosmic chef who knew only two recipes: priest and nun. Neither was all that exciting to me, and either way there was no sex involved.

To Kate, God was a kind of celestial Mister Rogers. Taking off his jacket so he could put on a cardigan, chatting with strange finger puppets all the while asking you to be his neighbor. God was unctuous and boring. And more than a little creepy.

How Good Became Boring

If you ask a person how her spiritual life is going, get ready to hear something like this: "Well, I'm not [fill in the blank: patient, loving, generous] enough; and I wish I were doing more [fill in the blank: praying, serving, paying taxes]; and last night I slipped up and [fill in the blank: got drunk, cussed, lusted, lied]; and that was a mistake, and I haven't [fill in the blank: confessed, repented] yet."

We tend to equate loss of spiritual vitality with the "bad" things we keep doing. We keep getting wasted after work, lusting in front of the computer, and later we lie about it. In contrast, when we think we see a turn toward spiritual health, it almost always is linked to things we're *not doing*. We didn't drink, cuss, lust, lie, or laugh at an off-color joke. Consider what this says about our understanding of goodness and serving God and humanity. "I didn't mess up much today, so I'm improving. Honestly, I hardly did a thing all day."

The fact that we equate avoiding things with being good should bother us. It should reveal something about us that is really disturbing.

For most of us, this all goes back to childhood. When you were a kid and your mom told you to "be good," was she telling you to do something or not to do something? Chances are you never heard "be good" associated with activism. Being good had to do with restraint.

Or take another example: Through the centuries almost every child has gone up to his mom and said, "Mooooooooom...I'm bored." But never in the history of the world has a mom smiled sweetly, patted the child on the head, and said, "The remedy to your problem is...to be good."

Nope. That doesn't work. That little sucker was already being good. That's why he's bored.

The wholesale promotion of doing nothing and calling it "good" has brought us to where we are today. The measure of goodness falls right in the average range. *Good* has become synonymous with *mediocre.* Goodness is boring; it's the essence of pulling back from the world, raising the drawbridge, and being isolated from most of what is going on in life.

This would be funny if it weren't so destructive. The redefinition of *good* as boring has distorted our understanding of God. As all religious folk know: "God is good." So what does that mean in practical terms?

If good is boring, and God is good, then God is boring. Most of us would not state it quite like that, but this is what many of us have been taught. And this is the spirituality that Kate was not interested in.

She was taught that the path to goodness involved mostly weeding out evil. But even if you could (in theory) weed out all the evil in your life, you would not have created something good. You would simply have created something *not* evil.

And when we translate this weeding idea to our everyday lives, being "not evil" can be just as dangerous as evil.

Creating Spiritual Vacuums

The word *vacuum* comes from a Latin word that means "empty." In physics a vacuum is created when there's an empty space with less atmospheric pressure inside the space than outside. When this happens, our universe's natural tendency is to fill that space with anything it can.

Take drinking a chocolate shake through a straw. When you suck on a straw, you suck air out of the straw. That's the first element of a vacuum. Element two is what happens next. Devoid of air, the space inside the straw has to be filled with something, and chocolate shake is really the only thing that's available. So, *bam!* The shake moves up the straw and into, you guessed it, your mouth.

Jesus, in fact, told this bizarre story about spiritual vacuums. He talked about what happens when something horrible is dislodged and cast out of a human soul. He called it an "unclean" spirit or force. Along with that you could include the removal of destructive choices and habits from a person's life. Essentially, Jesus was describing the spiritual physics that exist when we try to clean up our lives.

So we remove the debris left behind by our less-than-admirable choices and actions. Jesus said that when we remove these things, the unclean spirit searches for rest apart from us but doesn't find it. So the spirit we tossed out wanders around a while but eventually comes back. It says, in effect, "I will return to the soul I left." We've now gotten rid of a lot of bad choices or habits in our lives. We threw away some stuff or had some hard conversations or changed the way we interact with that certain someone and we're feeling pretty good.

And this, Jesus says, is when we're the most vulnerable.

The way Jesus tells the story is that the spirit goes around and finds some other unclean spirits that are even more wicked than itself, and they all come back with vigor. This gang of unsavory evil invades our souls, and now we're worse off than we were before.

It is a terrifying story.[1]

Now, you don't have to buy the spiritual worldview to see the principle for change. Jesus is explaining what happens when we try to clean up without filling up. It's what happens when we try to rid our lives of evil without filling our lives full of good.

When we remove destructive influences and patterns, a spiritual vacuum is created. Our hearts are made to be full, and our attention is designed to be occupied. So if we empty ourselves of evil but don't fill ourselves with something else, we become a kind of magnet for

destructive energy, a sponge-like sucking in of influences and attitudes and assumptions that will make our lives worse than before.

I'm convinced this is why so many people fail, even when they work
overtime to clean up their lives. They fixate on expelling negative influences, but they don't fill their lives with anything beautiful.

Good is not the absence of evil; it is the opposite of evil. When we define *good* as the absence of evil, we set ourselves up for failure.
Worse, we set ourselves up for average.

The Evil of Average[2]

One of the most provocative moments you can read in the scriptures
is that story mentioned earlier about the wise venture capitalist. The
man was going on a long trip and wanted to invest in three young
guys to see if they had the chops to lead and create. He gave each one
money to invest, and he gave the largest amount—five talents—to
the most promising of the three. To the middle guy he gave two talents, and the rookie got one talent. Then, like a good VC, he left town.
A long time later he came back to see what the kids had done.

The first guy, probably a college dropout with a flair for computers
and design, said, "I took your money and made a device that's a phone,
a computer, and a media player. And it's smaller than a deck of cards.
I doubled your money. Here's ten talents."

The second guy said pretty much the same thing. "I got into digital
reading devices, created a few hot apps, sold off the start-up to
Google. I doubled your money; here's four talents."

The third guy said, "I knew how demanding you are and that you'd probably punish me if I made a mistake. Besides, you only gave me one talent, which isn't as much as what the other guys got. So I buried your investment over there in the park so nothing would happen to it. Here's a treasure map. Dig it up yourself."

What's interesting about this story is the venture capitalist's response. He said, "You lazy, wicked servant."

That's pretty harsh. Most of us, as we're reading the story, are like "Yeah. The one-talent guy is a total jerk. He just dug a hole and stuck in the money." But think again about what the VC said. He called the failed entrepreneur a "lazy, wicked servant."

I can understand the lazy part. Lazy people don't do anything. This guy didn't do anything. Lazy = not doing anything. Got it.

But wicked?

I mean, if he had used the money to create the housing bubble debacle—artificially driving up real estate prices by selling subprime loans—yeah, that would be wicked. If he had started a sleazy magazine that objectifies women or had financed meth labs in Kentucky, that would be wicked.

But he didn't do any of those things. He didn't even lose the money— he just buried it. No crime was committed. He made what he considered the safest move of all: he did nothing.[3]

And in that bright, shining moment, Jesus redefined *average* as evil.

You see most of us, in our mind's system of measuring good and evil, create a Continuum of Virtue that looks something like this:

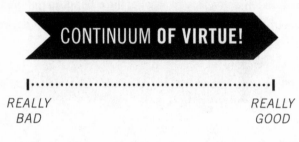

PART 1

We have "really bad" behavior on the left and "really good" on the right. (In this context, left and right are not connected to any kind of political statement, in case you were wondering.) Every choice we make can be plotted on this continuum. Killing someone because you don't like the way she looks? To the left. Inventing a kind of grain that transforms the agricultural landscape of India? To the right.

Here's my question: Where is the third entrepreneur on this continuum? He didn't lose the VC's money, so his actions would be somewhere in the middle, right? Not too bad and not too good. He'd be in the "average" zone. Like this:

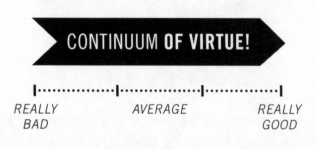

PART 2

Now, let's look at how the continuum tracks our own choices and behavior. Most of the time when we're trying to increase our "good" decisions, we might divide up the Continuum of Virtue. Everything that's "good" goes in the elongated box like this:

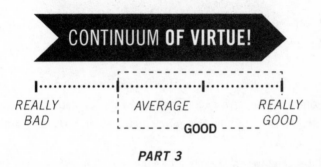

PART 3

Anything that lands near the "really good" end of the scale is good, as well as anything in the middle, or "average." Both are good. Meanwhile, "bad" is all the stuff that isn't "average" or "good."

But when Jesus called Entrepreneur Number 3 "wicked," He shifted this whole continuum. He drew a long box around evil that looks like this:

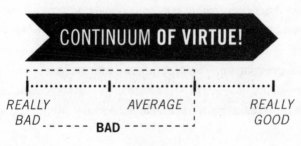

PART 4

See where Jesus puts "average"? It does not fall midway between really good and really bad. It is way over in the really bad territory.

This is enough to give us pause. Apparently, simply doing nothing is more wicked than we can imagine.

Good is not the absence of evil; it is the opposite of evil.

Good is not average. Good is not mediocre. Good is not boring. Good is not static, or inert, or sitting there in neutral.

Good is a *force.* It is not tame; it will tear through you like a freight train and rip your arm sockets off if you try to grab hold of it while standing still. That's why you gotta run to get on the Good Train.

Good has a texture and taste all its own—it's compelling and inspiring. Good will turn the world upside down.

When God Makes Us Boring

So how is it that well-meaning people ruined the risky goodness of God with a boring picture of God? And why did people of faith, by and large, accept this corruption of God's goodness? Here's what I think.

For a few years I was highly involved in a partnership between a Los Angeles faith community—Mosaic, and Golden Gate Theological Seminary outside San Francisco. We affectionately named this effort the Protégé Program.[4] The program included dozens of young leaders from all over the world who became part of the Mosaic community and received a master of theology degree from the seminary at the same time.

One of my roles was to serve on the interview board to help screen potential protégés as they arrived in Los Angeles to experience the community for the first time. I will never forget one of the gentlemen we interviewed. He was such a nice guy, but when we asked him questions, it seemed that nothing would light his fire. The Protégé Program only worked for the deeply motivated. Participants had to come with a fire and almost a sense of rebelliousness against the system to survive the program. This guy didn't have it.

We wrapped up the interview; then as we were walking into the night-club where Mosaic was meeting, this guy paused and mentioned, sheepishly, "Hey, uh... There's something I forgot to put on my application."

"Oh yeah?" I said.

"Yeah, it asked if I've ever been involved in any illegal activity. I put 'no.' Well, that's not exactly true."

My ears perked up. Maybe we were finally getting somewhere.

"Yeah. Uh, well, when I was in high school, I used to steal from local stores and then sell the merchandise at a discounted cost to my friends."

He looked down, ashamed. "It kind of helped pay for college."

Now that's interesting.

This guy, when he was seventeen, was involved in the black market and was highly successful. He pursued his entrepreneurial talent (albeit immorally) and became his town's Al Capone. (Sounds a lot like a guy from the scriptures named Matthew. You know, the guy who wrote the Gospel According to Matthew? He was involved with organized crime.)

"What happened to all those skills you had in high school?" I asked.

He beamed with pride. "Oh, when I started following Jesus, I stopped all that."

My heart sank. He had stopped stealing, but what had he started doing in its place?

For some reason this young man threw the entrepreneurial baby out with the black-market bath water. This is what happens when good goes bad.

EIGHT

Embracing Inspired Living

////////////

The questionable recruiting of God

It might be hard to accept, but God did not choose traditionally good people to lead His movement of beauty in the world. He picked the terrorists, the morally corrupt, the passionately wrong. Granted, He invited these people to become moral and to experience the thrill and challenge of integrity. But read the scriptures and you'll see that God prefers to set the wrong on the right path than to keep shouting "Move!" to the safe souls who have trouble leaving the sidelines for the playing field.

God almost never pushes. He invites. He didn't push Moses. (But he did push Pharaoh, who resisted God's plan with everything he had. God pushed him like the plague.) Yet God's overwhelming preference is to *guide*. It is true that in the scriptures God commanded people to wait. But when He issued a command of restraint, He usually was dealing with those who found it *hard* to wait.

The scriptures are full of folks who have a hard time waiting, and God keeps telling them to slow down. King David was an action-oriented dude. All the prophets were a little, you know, crazy. Those who are at the forefront of what God is doing in the world are there because they enjoy nothing better than something risky.

To the ones who are looking for action and tend to get ahead of God, He oftentimes has to say, "Be patient. Not yet."

So if you're always on the move, then "wait" might be God's message for you right now. Yet if you're always "on the wait," then "move" might be a little more relevant.

I'm worried that we've taken a theology of "waiting on the Lord" and have used it to justify a debilitating reticence, a stultifying tendency to stand by, immobile, anchored to safety. You say "Whoa!" to a horse that's out of control, not to the one that's lying dead in the stable.

Think about Jesus's first followers. Peter was a passionate man who often was passionately wrong. Taking up swords, cutting off ears.

Simon was a Zealot. Zealots were terrorists. Terrorists can be accused of a lot of things, but never of lacking passion.

Matthew was a corrupt businessman. A sleazy ambulance chaser of a sellout, cheating his own people to benefit a conquering government and putting the leftovers in his own silk-lined pockets.

James and John were greedy, power-hungry young leaders who kept asking their mom, of all people, to ask Jesus if they could be in charge after He established His new kingdom.

These men and others who would never be nominated for Citizen of the Year were handpicked by Jesus. They were not so-called "good people." If you tried to bring them home to meet Mom and Dad, your parents would lock the doors and pretend they weren't there. Jesus's closest comrades were guys who would inspire you to sneak out of the house late at night to go joyriding in a hot-wired car. These guys are why decent citizens carry a can of Mace.

All of this is why the next thought should be at least a little disturbing: Jesus picked the people that we teach our children to avoid. He picked rough characters to be His messengers of compassion to the ends of the earth. He picked the jerks, the bullies, and the gothic kid in the back row who keeps setting things on fire and has the symbol for anarchy drawn in indelible ink on his hand.

Jesus rounded up the kids who flushed cherry bombs down the toilets at school and set mice loose on the floor of the commons between third and fourth period (true story). They were morally idiotic but intuitively creative. They were looking for action. And to them Jesus said, "Follow me."

He overlooked the goody-goodies, the ones who had it all together. The ones who would rather get it right than create something beautiful. The ones who got angry when Jesus ignored their moral GPAs.

The story goes that a president of Harvard was giving a speech to other college presidents. "Take care of your A+ students," he encouraged. "They will come back and make fine professors someday.

"Take better care of your D+ students," he concluded. "For they will come back and donate $4 million to your new building program."

Jesus picked D students. They're the ones who aren't terrified of getting a wrong answer, which means they're free to roam around and discover new answers. They're the ones who aren't busy figuring out how to exploit the system because, if they point themselves in the right direction, they'll create their own system. They can spot irrelevance in a New York minute. They hate playing games. They have a limited tolerance for authority.

In short, they are leaders.

They are more interested in making a difference than following rules. They'd rather do something meaningful, but imperfectly, than something meaningless but without error.

They are not afraid of making mistakes. In fact, of all the things you see people afraid of in the scriptures, making a mistake is almost never mentioned. Yet that is what prevents so many of us from doing any good at all.

The movement of God wasn't meant to be perfect; it was meant to be inspiring.

The Power of Inspiration

I used to hate running more than just about anything else. My dad taught me a lot of valuable life lessons, and the one that stuck with me more than most was this: you never see a happy runner.

Think about it. On Sunday mornings you see joggers out there chugging along the side of the road, and they don't look happy. They look like they're in pain. At best it looks like they're trying to do complex math problems in their heads.

Or think about the Olympics. The guy who wins the race knows he'll be getting a gold medal, but he looks like somebody just came along and ripped off one of his toenails. I don't know whether to cheer or call an ambulance.

So I don't mind telling you that I hate running. I could easily make a list—a long list—of things I'd rather do than run.

A few years ago I read an article about a guy named Dean Karnazes. Dean is an ultramarathon runner. (An ultramarathon is anything over seventy miles.) Dean has run fifty marathons in all fifty states. One time he ran from Southern California to New York.

Karnazes is a living, breathing Forrest Gump.

He ran the 135-mile Badwater ultramarathon through Death Valley in 120-degree heat. It was so hot that if you didn't run on the white line in the middle of the road, your shoes would melt. A car drove next to each runner, and the driver would roll down the side window to give the assigned runner a piece of bread. While the window was down, the bread would toast.

My favorite story about Dean is that eleven times he has run a 199-mile relay race, often solo, competing against teams of twelve people each, and he has finished ahead of some teams.

Can you imagine being on one of the teams that finished behind him? You're at the finish line, bent over and breathing heavily after having completed one-twelfth of a 199-mile race. And you're unhappy (first of all, because you were running—but you have other reasons besides that one).

"Hey, Bill," you say to one of your eleven teammates.

"Yeah, Larry."

"Which team beat us?" you ask.

Between gasping for breath and squirting water in his face from a bright plastic bottle with a logo on it, Bill points off to the left. There stands Dean.

"That guy, over there," says Bill.

When I was first exposed to Dean's story, I immediately knew that Dean is some kind of awesome.[1] Now, as I mentioned before, I hate running. I'll do pretty much anything I can to avoid it. But after I heard about Dean, I started looking for the nearest pair of running shoes.

You see, there's something inspiring when we see people push themselves past what any of us thought was possible. My whole life I've been impressed by the best. I love watching John Mayer shred a guitar solo. A friend of mine was his RA in college, and I've loved listening to stories of John not going to class and annoying everyone in the dorm because of his incessant playing.

I love seeing amazing dance. Amazing physical prowess. I love watching Bill Cosby or Jerry Seinfeld do stand-up. They make it look so easy.

I love going to Da Poetry Lounge in West Hollywood (Dapoetrylounge .com). On any given Tuesday night, you'll find some of the best spoken-word poets in the world performing for a packed house— speaking, laughing, crying, inspiring an audience with art that leaves you breathless.

I loved watching Harry Connick Jr. perform a few years back at the Hollywood Bowl. That guy can play just about every instrument and— quite simply—knows how to entertain. He takes an audience of twenty thousand and makes each person feel like he or she is in a living room just chillin' with Harry while he plays the piano.

When people such as Harry Connick Jr. and John Mayer and Jerry Seinfeld and poets at Da Poetry Lounge do what they do, it makes me want to do what I do.

They inspire me.

So what does this have to do with us connecting with God? Turns out, everything.

The Voice(s) of God

I've always struggled to hear God's voice. Honestly, it feels like I have twenty people in my mind arguing with one another. Most of the time I kind of enjoy it, since some of these people are pretty entertaining. But when it comes to hearing the voice of God, it's hard to know which of the voices, if any, is His.

Usually when we're asking to hear the voice of God, what we really want is to know His will. We want Him to tell us what to do or if what we're doing is okay or if there's something we're not doing that we should be doing or if there's something we're doing that we shouldn't be doing.

Sometimes the scriptures are helpful. Sometimes we're so angry that we want to hurt someone and the scriptures say, "Yeah, that's not a good idea."[2] So we don't. Hooray for the will of God! But other times it's not as black or white. When it comes to knowing the will of God, it's often hard to even know where to start.

How can I know what the will of God is? It's not like there's a verse that says, "This is the will of God for your life..."

Except there is.

Seriously.

I was so excited when I found it about ten years ago. I couldn't believe no one had ever told me about it. (It says, "This is the will of God for your life...")

But then what came next disappointed me a little. There is nothing about performing tremendous feats of strength or speaking before thousands. Here is how one Bible translation says it: "It is God's will that you should be sanctified."[3]

Another translation says it this way: "God's will is for you to be holy."[4]

Holy? Sanctified? Snooze button.

The word *holiness* literally means "to be set apart." It means "to be different."

When I was growing up, I was taught that being different meant we didn't do what I now call the Big Five:

1. Don't smoke.
2. Don't cuss.
3. Don't watch bad movies.
4. Don't have sex.
5. Don't hang out with bad people (as defined by numbers 1 through 4 above).

And the unspoken number six on the list was "Go to church."

If you could excel at these five or six things, you qualified as a "good person." You were holy. Different from everyone else, the ones who cuss while they smoke like a factory and like to have sex after getting home from attending an R-rated movie.

Now please, don't misunderstand me: The point here is not whether the list is good or bad. It's just that it's a woefully incomplete and boring list.

So when I read that God's will for me was...to be "holy," that didn't really do it for me. But as I grew older, my definition of holiness began to change.

I began meeting people who lived incredible lives. I met folks who were faithful to their wives *and* who trained leaders in Africa to start nonprofits that funded orphanages for children with AIDS.

I met people who ran companies that devoted large portions of their profits to humanitarian causes.

I met models in Hollywood who treated the women they dated with respect and dignity. And I met people who had incredible relationships. I know people who are creative not just in the arts but also in their generosity to others. They live lives of adventure...of goodness... of holiness.

In short, I began meeting people who inspired me. They inspired me not only in what they abstained from but also in what they *engaged in.* They loved life.

It was intoxicating.

Since then the word *holiness* has taken on new meaning. For me, it means "inspiring."

In the scriptures when God called people to holiness, He wasn't insisting they adhere to a list of arbitrary rules that would make them different or strange. It wasn't a call to be odder than thou; it was a call to a beautiful and difficult way of living. God was calling people to live inspiring lives.

The word *inspired* comes from the Latin word *inspirare*, which means "to set aflame, to blow into."

To spark.

When God formed Adam out of the earth in the Garden of Pleasure and breathed life into him, God was inspiring him. When you begin sparking your life, your life becomes a fire—full of life. Full of God.

You were designed to live an inspiring life.

This is the will of God: for you to live an inspiring life. A spark to become a light in the darkness. To drink deeply of God and become a well of life for others.

And, generally speaking, there are an infinite number of ways to make this happen.

In one letter written to a community in the city of Philippi, Paul of Tarsus wrote that we should give ourselves to "whatever is true, whatever is honorable, whatever is just, whatever is pure, whatever is lovely, whatever is commendable, if there is any excellence, if there is anything worthy of praise."[5]

Paraphrase? Devote your attention and energy to things that are inspiring, because those are the things of God. And when you do this, you'll begin experiencing God in ways you never would have predicted.

When I hear about Dean Karnazes, it inspires me to run. Other people inspire me to forgive, to be vulnerable about my dreams for the future. When I see anyone meet life at the intersection of what's difficult and beautiful, it takes my breath away...and then breathes life back into me.

So the question I will ask you is: What's stopping you from living a more inspirational life?

On Passion

Dean once told an interviewer: "Somewhere along the line, we seem to have confused comfort with happiness."[6]

I meet people who say, "I'm passionate about so many things"—film, music, dance, video games, education, traveling, collecting stamps, reading, writing. The sky is the limit to people's passion. But what does it mean to be passionate about something?

When people describe their passions, they almost always talk about something they dabble in. Or it's something they're excited about. Often people's "passions" are things they do from time to time, when they can find the time. It's what they do because they love it, not because they get paid to do it. It's fun for them.

What's interesting is that the word *passion* is taken from a Greek word that means "to suffer." This is why the last hours of Jesus's life are called "the passion of the Christ." It's not because Jesus was super excited to be executed. Jesus didn't just dabble in redemption when He had a little time to spare. Roman crucifixion wasn't fun. It was because He was willing to suffer for the sake of humanity.

You know you're passionate about something when you're willing to suffer for it.

When my friend Rosanna, who plays water polo for the Canadian Women's National Team, gets up every morning before 6 a.m. to swim, lift, sweat, and generally punish her body in an effort to be the strongest, most agile athlete in the water, you know she is passionate about making it to the Olympics.

When my friend Mateo moved to Los Angeles and ate beans from a can, living in a small studio apartment so that someday he could go on to write the Grammy-winning score to the Academy Award–winning *Juno*, you know he is passionate about composing music.

Their passion is not a masochistic, joyless passion. And their joy is deeper than any fleeting moment. The denial of present pleasures pales in comparison to the thrill of being an Olympic athlete or an award-winning composer. Incidentally, the word *apathy* means, literally, to have "no passion." It is a life with no suffering. So when we seek to have a life involving no suffering, what we are asking for is a life of apathy.

Is that really what you and I want? Is that the "good life"?

Let's talk more about goodness, and how spreading good in the world is the life that most fully expresses what it means to be alive.

NINE

Good Is Everywhere

/////////

How to see what God is doing. How to step into it

The human brain is limited to focusing on approximately 128 bits of information at one moment. Yet we are bombarded by 2 to 4 million bits of information at a time. At any given moment we are unaware of around 3 million bits of information, or ninety-nine percent of what is happening around us.[1]

We're never seeing the whole picture.

Following is one of my favorite exercises to illustrate this. Gaze at the illustration,[2] then close your right eye and focus your attention on the X. Now hold the book (or tablet screen) close to your face and, while keeping one eye closed and the other focused on the X, slowly move the illustration away from your face until the dot on the left disappears.

Weird, isn't it? There is a physical space in the back of your eye that contains no photoreceptors. (That is the place where all the optic nerves—the eye's cables—leave the eye. Kind of like where a power cord leaves a hanging lamp.) Since there are no photoreceptors there, you can't see certain things.

You might be wondering, "If I can't see it, then why isn't there a noticeable gap all the time in my field of vision? Right now, I'm reading your words just fine, and I don't see a blank spot."

Great point. Why is that?

Your brain looks at the surrounding area and *infers* what belongs in the blind spot based on what's around it. Since there is white space surrounding the dot in the illustration we used, that's what your brain guesses should belong inside the blind spot.

Not only can we not see certain things, but we also fill in our blind spots with what we can see. Or as Anais Nin once said, "We don't see things as they are, we see them as we are."[3] We're constantly guessing at what we can't see using what we think we see as a starting point.

What do you see when you look at the world around you? When you go to bed at night, what kind of world do you see waiting for you in the morning? Is it hostile? inviting? boring? interesting? overwhelming? exciting?

There was a season of my life—years, actually—when I would wake up every morning and do the same thing. I'd turn on the shower, collapse on my knees, and, if I could muster the energy, cry. What I felt was overwhelming fear, depression, and sadness.

What I saw was certain failure and hopelessness. I saw every mistake I was making. I saw everything I didn't like about my life.

And what about the parts of the day, and my future, that I *couldn't* see?

My soul was filling in the blanks with despair. Just like your brain fills in for your eyes' blind spot, my lens on life was supplying me with additional desperation. When fear and sadness are all you can see, that is what you will infer in the parts of your life that you can't see.

The world felt so heavy. My heart ached for reasons I couldn't articulate. And here's what is crazy: a majority of the ache came from things that weren't real. The ache was caused by my tainted lens filling in the gaps of my life with "realities" that weren't rooted in reality.

That's the power of the lenses through which we see life. They shape how we see ourselves, how we see others, how we see God, how we see our place in the world. Our lenses re-create reality in their image. Meanwhile, they blind us to things that are really there. They blind us to the dot inside the rectangle that is right in front of each of our faces. Sometimes this dot can be a character flaw or some serious issue in our lives that we're unaware of.

But most of the time, the dot is something beautiful, something good, something hopeful that's right in front of us. We could see it if we'd only have the eyes to see it.

Living the Jenga Life

One of my spiritual mentors used to despise the word *balance*. More than once I heard him say, "We've learned more about spirituality

from Mr. Miyagi in *The Karate Kid* than from Jesus." Any time someone would ask how my mentor balanced his life, he would first reject
the premise that balance was one of his goals.

What he was railing against was the idea that moderation is always a
good thing. If balance refers to equilibrium, it puts the focus on the
middle of the seesaw. That view of balance cancels out both ends and
emphasizes the boring middle. Not too passionate, not too dead, but
somewhere in between. Average, mediocre, balance. In this view,
balance is like a giant cosmic game of Jenga. All the pieces are in
place, perfectly still. But if you remove one block the wrong way, the
whole thing collapses.

Game over.

Playing Jenga is stressful. It's all about not making mistakes. Every
move has to be delicate, perfect. It's as if they took all the horrifying
elements involved in dismantling a bomb and put it into a game for
families to enjoy. Whatever you do, don't make the tower fall. Yet every
move makes the tower sway. I wonder how many times I've lost at
Jenga due more to my anxiety of losing than any block that I pulled out.
If you put too much effort into seeking balance, you lose the game.

When I hear "balance," I think of school children with their arms outstretched, each standing on one foot. I think of a nurse delicately tap-
ping a sliding weight on a scale to see how much you weigh when you
go in for a physical.

What is shared in common by all these images is that they're static.
They're not moving. A child isn't moving when she is balancing with
arms stretched wide and standing on one foot. That's the point: if she
moved, she would fall. The scale at the doctor's office isn't moving.

Your weight, balanced against the scale's weight, holds the bar stationary. If the scale moved around, it wouldn't be called a "scale" but a "ride," and we'd probably enjoy going to the doctor more.

In the same way, the Jenga blocks, if you play well, remain perfectly still.

Still. Static. Dead.

Don't touch anything and the tower stands. Touch anything and the whole thing collapses.

When there is this kind of pressure in life, the most attractive option can often be to not risk making a move. But when you stop moving, you stop living. Your dreams begin to fade, but worse than that, your imagination—the place where dreams are born—begins to weaken.

Imaginations can atrophy just like muscles. There's a saying in neurophysiology: "If you don't use it, you lose it." That's why senior citizens work crossword puzzles. It keeps their brains active. The same is true of dreaming, imagining, and solving problems.

I used to look at my life with God that way. In fact, I used to read the Garden of Eden that way. As though God were being such a buzzkill when He told Adam and Eve not to eat fruit from one of the trees in the garden, the Tree of the Knowledge of Good and Evil.

If we were to apply the Jenga model of spirituality to the Garden of Eden, it might look like this. Imagine a game of Jenga with one million blocks. Each Jenga block is approximately 1.5 x 2.5 x 7.5 centimeters, about the size of a candy bar. If the base were three blocks wide (standard in this game), then a game of Jenga using one million blocks would stand approximately three miles high. By way of comparison, the tallest building in North America is Chicago's Willis Tower at seventeen hundred feet, less than one-third of a mile.

So our one-million-block Jenga game would be about the height of ten Willis Towers stacked on top of one another.

Now, imagine that each block represents something beautiful, something magical and creative that Adam (getting back to our story) will absolutely love. There's a block labeled "Give Eve a big kiss." And another block is labeled "Go skinny-dipping." Another invites the couple to "Have an amazing conversation about your dreams for the future." Each block, except for one, is something good. There is one block that's painted dark red. It's the *bad* block. In the book of Genesis, we're told that God said to Adam, *You can touch any of the one million blocks you want except the red one. You can kick the tower, juggle the blocks, have a ball. Feel free to take out whole rows of blocks; you'll see that the tower won't fall. But don't touch the red block.*

There would still be 999,999 really attractive blocks, and Adam and Eve could do anything with any or all those blocks without upsetting the tower.

If those were the rules of the game, how would that change the way we play? And how would it affect the way we see not just the game, but all of life?

If everything around our blind spots is possibility, then we will fill in the unknown areas, the empty spaces and our blind spots, with more possibility. The unknowns and uncertainties will no longer attract dark images of fear or failure. They will be overwhelmed by new possibilities.

Granted, there are more red blocks now than there were in the Garden of Eden. But even now, there are more good blocks than bad blocks.

So what do we see when we look at the world: 999,999 good blocks or one red block? Do we see the one hundred things we could do today that would be fulfilling, beautiful, and noble, or do we see the five things that would be destructive? And after noticing the five destructive possibilities, do we stop doing anything for fear we might slip up and grab on to a red block?

Developing a Lens of Opportunity

What would it look like if we began developing a lens of opportunity—opportunity to live, to risk, and to serve others? Opportunities are hiding in every conversation, in every relationship. These are the hidden blocks of beauty that beckon us to more rewarding lives. These are the oftentimes small and sometimes large-yet-unseen opportunities that God places in our path. We need only to develop eyes that are ready to see opportunities.

With Spark Groups, when we ask the question "What's one risk you can take to make yourself a better person or the world a better place?" we're asking participants to flex their imagination the same way they would flex a muscle. It's an invitation to begin cultivating a lens of opportunity rather than a lens of negativity.

Embedded in the question are more specific questions, such as:

- **What does it look like** to be an incredible son or daughter?
- **What does it take** to start really caring about the hurting and the broken?

- **What would it mean** for you to admit that you are hurting and broken, and to put yourself in environments where you can heal?
- **What would it take** for you to make a relationship you care about a little bit better, or even to take a leap and make it a lot better?
- **What does it look like** to use your finances in more compassionate ways?

Answering these questions will lead you to the extraordinary choices that will make your life more meaningful. The choices will lead to risks that will move you outside the status quo, where you can step into something new.

Remember the Continuum of Virtue from chapter 7? Most of us tend to look at the continuum like this:

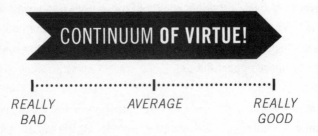

CONTINUUM **OF VIRTUE!**

REALLY BAD   *AVERAGE*   *REALLY GOOD*

That's what we looked at in chapter 7. But the scriptures seem to indicate that the continuum really looks like this:

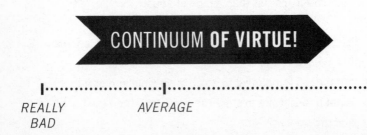

CONTINUUM **OF VIRTUE!**

REALLY BAD   *AVERAGE*

There's more good than there is bad. And the range of good is far wider than the range of bad. We just aren't always aware of it.

Redefining *Balance* as Movement

So what are we to think about balance? If it doesn't mean settling into the middle, what *does* it mean?

Zac Woodfin and I became friends when Zac was training athletes who were about to be drafted into the NFL. Today Zac is a strengths and conditioning coach for the Green Bay Packers, one of the most respected teams in all of football.

When Zac thinks about balance, he doesn't think about something that is stable and perfectly still. To him, balance is a 250-pound man running at high speed, constantly shifting his center of gravity so he can evade other 250-pound men who are out there trying to stop him.

"Balance is fluid," Zac told me. "It's control but in a dynamic environment. If you can stay standing up while standing in place, I guess that's great," he said, laughing. "But that's not sport. That's not life."

To athletes, balance is important. But not in a Jenga-be-careful-don't-touch-anything way. Balance is the constantly shifting re-evaluation of yourself to keep yourself upright and moving. Balance becomes an act of reflection as you move forward in an ever-changing world.

Balance takes into account that life is change and movement. The more you move, the more important balance becomes.

This new view of balance brings us back to the first question of Spark Groups: What's one risk you can take this week to make you a better person or the world a better place? It's a straightforward question that forces you to reflect on who you want to be and what kind of world you want to create. It helps you to recalibrate, to rebalance your values and priorities, and to begin taking sometimes small, sometimes large steps in new directions. Answering the question moves you toward balance by moving you to the places you want to go. It helps you become the person you long to be.

It's a question you must constantly be asking, just as an athlete is constantly paying attention to his body and shifting his balance as he keeps moving. Asking this question not only helps you rebalance your life, but it also begins to help you change the lens through which you see the world. If you ask the Spark question on a regular basis, you will start to see opportunities where you once saw obstacles. Your everyday world will gradually turn into a playground of possibility where every moment is a potential moment to serve someone.

When you seek true balance in your life, every day will offer an opportunity to do something that's at least a little bit courageous.

TEN

The Posture of Risk

///////////

How to move forward without losing your balance

Submission is not my generation's favorite word. Really, the people who like that word are usually in charge of something. Nobody who has to follow orders really likes to submit. But when you think about it, we all submit to something or someone. Olympic athletes submit to the rigorous training that athletic excellence requires, teaching their bodies to do the impossible. Musicians submit to hours of practice in order to perform at their peak level.

Athletes, musicians, and others submit their immediate feelings and desires to the requirements necessary to achieve their long-term goals.

And even "ordinary" people who don't compete or perform at world-class level submit to something. A friend once said, "I submit to no man." Sounds so tough, doesn't it? But what people mean when they say that is that they submit only to their constantly changing subconscious desires.

I know what it's like to submit to how I'm feeling. If the alarm goes off in the morning and I feel tired, I roll over and submit to the feeling of sleepiness. If I feel hungry when driving past a fast-food establish-ment, I pull into the drive-through lane and submit to a burger. Maybe you've experienced this too. If we don't want to work, we call in sick. If telling the truth would be embarrassing or inconvenient, we tell a lie. If doing the right thing would hurt, then we do the wrong thing instead.

In those moments we're not just submitting to something; we're sub-mitting to *the most foolish thing:* ourselves. Submitting to ourselves is the only form of submission that requires no humility. And that is probably what makes it evil.

The question is not whether we're submitting. The question is, Can we *trust* what we're submitting to? I've been in relationships with people who were not trustworthy. When I realized I could no longer trust them, I got out of those relationships. And if circumstances pre-vented me from leaving completely, I put a healthy amount of dis-tance between us. I will not continue to submit myself to an untrustworthy person if I can help it.

Of course, some people *are* trustworthy. At least they try really hard to be, and when they mess up, they apologize. I know leaders, friends, and family who have ability and great wisdom and are—frankly— worth submitting to.

And beyond the people who inspire trust, there are beautiful ideals that you will largely miss out on unless you are willing to submit. Ideas like integrity, beauty, goodness, and joy. These ideals are worth submitting to.

It's not natural to answer to someone else or to set aside your own plans in order to work for the success of another person's plans. But when we submit to these ideals, our lives begin to take on a texture that is life giving. The process of submission may not feel good, but the end result that submission produces is nothing less than extraordinary. Submitting your personal desires and feelings to the task of accomplishing something greater is an act that builds your character, and your life, in amazing ways.

You can't create a thing that is morally beautiful if you submit only to how you feel. You and I can become who we long to be only when we submit to something greater than ourselves. Risking for something greater than ourselves is always an act of submission. It requires us to say that what we've chosen is more important than our feelings, preferences, fears, or hurts. The word *submission* means to "put yourself under a mission." You have to lower yourself if you want to do something greater than yourself.

The Power of Lowering Yourself

My friend Zac taught me that if you want to move fast and change direction while maintaining speed, you have to stay low. You can run fast standing up (in the style of a sprinter), but you can't change direction like that. If you're a ball carrier and you want to cut and juke to make tacklers miss, you have to stay low. You have to submit to a low center of gravity.

I believe there is a correlation between the physical nature of movement and the spiritual nature of humility. If you want to move fast, you have to stay low.

We see this hinted at brilliantly in the Hebrew scriptures. The story goes that God called Abram to leave everything he knew in Haran and set out for Canaan. The place name *Haran* has the implied meaning of "high." As a personal name it means "Mountaineer." *Canaan* means "lowland" and it comes from the same root word as the Hebrew word for "humble." When God called Abram to leave his home in Haran, God was calling him to go from a high place to a low place.

When Abram stepped away from his culture, his religion, and his extended family to look for a strange land, he was going from a high place to a low place. He was taking a step from arrogance to humility, from knowledge to faith, and from certainty to trust.[1]

We take a similar journey when we set out from the familiar life we've been leading to seek out growth and change. It's often a long, meandering, unclear journey from arrogance to humility. From running tall to the more exciting and adventurous act of staying low. We lower our spiritual centers of gravity so we can duck and weave, making quick changes in direction.

The first year we launched Spark Good, I thought we were set. I had some great leads with huge organizations in Los Angeles and in other parts of the country. Those deals were going to provide security for the company for the first year, and I was looking forward to ramping things up.

Then all the deals fell through. Every single one. I didn't know what to do, and I had a lot of time on my hands to consider all that I didn't know. I was angry with myself, and I was angry with God.

I had wanted to sprint. I had wanted to stand tall and run in one direction. Then one day I sensed God say, *Jason, did you start this company to make money or to help people?*

Help people, I grumbled.

Well, then, He said, *go help somebody.* I spent that fall changing our strategy and utilizing our program and training capabilities in working with inner-city kids in East Los Angeles. We also worked in several homeless shelters throughout the city. We got to serve folks who couldn't afford to pay us for the help.

It was not a great business plan, but it's what we felt we needed to do. It required us to change—to take risks. If we were going to fulfill the mission God had given us, we had to submit to the opportunities He was presenting. We got low to invest in something greater than ourselves. The path of risk always involves humility.

How about you? What is in your life that is greater than yourself? What is the change that you sense you need to make—but you're struggling with it—because pride is getting in the way? What would it look like for you to humble yourself and make the change, this week or even today?

We help people form Spark Groups for a couple of reasons. One is that doing this sort of thing along with a small group of like-minded people makes it a lot more fun, more interesting, and more doable. But there is a second important reason, and it is this: when you tell your friends in a Spark Group what risk you're going to take, you're submitting. It's not that anyone in the group orders you to make a certain change in your life. It's that you are submitting to integrity—choosing to follow through with what you said you would do. You are submitting to the honor of choosing something beautiful rather than just doing what is comfortable. In a very real way, you're submitting to God.

When you join or create a Spark Group, you are creating a space that will help you and others lower their moral and spiritual centers of gravity to help them stay on their toes, to continue to develop the art of self-challenge, and to be balanced on your journey into a better future.

So Many Risks, So Little Time

Sometimes it's hard to know which risk to take. When we start looking for opportunities to make the world a better place, we see a world that is full of opportunities. And it can be overwhelming. How do you know where to start?

When our team works with different types of organizations, invariably they ask, "Where should we start? There are so many options." There have been times when we've revisited the same organization later on and they're still trying to figure out where to jump in. Don't become paralyzed when you see so many options, needs, and opportunities. Instead, take the advice I always offer: "Just ask her to dance."

Ask Her to Dance

Once upon a time there was a prince. When it came time for him to marry, he ordered his servants to search the land for the most beautiful, intelligent, talented, and deserving women.

After months of searching, the servants came back with one thousand single women from all over the world. They were the greatest leaders, the brightest minds, the most beautiful women the servants could find. All of them were far out of the prince's league, but he was a prince, so I guess he had that going for him.

The prince decided to have a ball where the women would be his royal guests. At the ball he would chose his bride. The same ritual had been followed for generations. The prince would walk into the ballroom, select a young woman, and ask her to dance. That would begin the courtship season, and if all went well the two would marry.

On the night of the ball, the prince arrived to see one thousand outstanding women from around the world, and he froze. Where to even begin?

He began moving toward one woman with his hand outstretched in invitation, but then stopped. What if another woman in this crowded ballroom was a more perfect match? He turned to see another woman, who smiled confidently. He began moving toward her, then froze again. How could he be sure *she* was the best and the brightest?

After an hour of worry and indecision, he left the ballroom, intending to give the matter more thought. He would defer a decision, so he could do more research! More pragmatically, he would get on with his daily life. After all, he was a busy man. The women probably weren't going anywhere (the royal guards would see to that). The prince could always decide on a partner some other time.

A year passed. The prince still had not made his decision. He kept the women waiting while he contemplated his decision.

Five years passed. Then twenty. And even after *seventy* years went by, the women were still waiting. Magically, they were still young and impressive and beautiful. Yet for fear of making the wrong choice, the prince never chose.

In the end he died alone. And the world's most beautiful, most gifted, most talented women remain, to this day, waiting to be chosen.

On Beautiful Causes

-

To me, this isn't a story about dating (although for some of you, it could be). For me, this is a story about choice. (And if you're offended by the story for its chauvinism, I understand.) I'm offended by the story too. *Mostly* because the prince could have chosen any of the women, without making them wait, and they would all have been out of his league. In his *not* choosing, he was communicating a clear message: not a single one of these outstanding choices was worth his time.

He valued a perfect choice over making a good choice and enjoying a life of fulfilling love. He valued his ideals over his options.

Some of you might admire the prince because he didn't want to settle. If you want the best in life, you should wait until the best makes itself clear.

Here's the problem with that: in the story, *all* the women were in the top one-half percent. Every one of them was worth this guy's time. Yet he still rejected them.

Many of us make the same mistake—not in who we date, but in how we live. There are, right now, more than one thousand worthy causes in the world. Beautiful causes. Meaningful causes. Important causes.

- **Expanding** access to education
- **Combating** disease
- **Alleviating** poverty
- **Protecting** the environment
- **Addressing** spiritual emptiness

These are beautiful choices. Each one is worthy. If each of these causes were an available single person, we'd be lucky to be with *any* of them. We don't have to make a lifetime commitment, but at least we could ask one to dance.

Ultimately that's what a Spark is: it's asking good to dance. It's not getting married to a worthy cause (most of the time it's not even a commitment to go out for a nice dinner and a movie afterward). It's just asking good to dance. And you don't have to wait until you're confident that you're making the perfect choice. It's about choosing *something*.

Here's what's exciting: at any given moment there are countless decisions, choices, and opportunities that exceed whatever it is you have settled for so far. Any one of these decisions would fall in line with the will of God. At any given moment God is presenting multiple options to you and asking, pleading, *Pick one.*

Right now you're reading these words, but you *could* be doing one of many other good things (and perhaps wish you were). You could be serving the poor or listening to a hurting friend or making a meal for an elderly couple down the street. You could be tutoring a child or demonstrating in support of civil rights. You could be writing an encouraging note or giving dignity to someone's questions about spirituality. The point isn't that you *should* be doing any or all of those things, just that you *could* be doing any of those things.

This moment is full of opportunity to ask good to dance.

But often, because we could do anything, we opt for doing nothing. In education it's called "the curse of the gifted." Pepperdine University, where I teach, attracts some of the brightest young minds in the world. They can pretty much do *anything they want*. Which is why they struggle with what to do with their lives. It's not the fear of mediocrity; it's the fear of missing out on everything else. Being afraid of missing out keeps us from jumping in, and jumping in is way more fun (and formative) than stressing over what to do.

When we begin to engage in the good we know we can be doing, we become aware of specific good that we are called to create in specific situations.

The Music of God

Oftentimes I'm in a restaurant and there's music playing. Then during a conversation my mind will drift toward the background music. What usually happens is I'll hear a hook that sounds familiar or a bass rhythm that I know I've heard before. All of a sudden it becomes a game of Name That Tune. I'll totally disconnect from the conversation and leverage all my sentient resources toward identifying the song. My body will instinctively connect with any part of the music I can grab on to. I'll tap my feet. I'll bob my head. I might not be able to discern the lyrics, but essentially I'm building the song in my imagination until it becomes clear.

This is similar to the way I hear the voice of God. I start with what I know and begin moving toward what I don't. I start with the general and begin moving toward the specific. Even if I can't hear the lyrics or identify the key, I can at least start moving my feet and bobbing my head to the beat that I *can* hear.

One time years ago I was talking with a friend named Ron. He was a stand-up comic, and he has one of the most charismatic personalities I've ever run into. While he lived in Los Angeles, he was one of my favorite friends. Ron was also antagonistic toward organized religion.

Whenever we would get together, we'd talk about work and relationships, but eventually the conversation would drift toward spirituality. Sometimes we'd argue, and sometimes we wouldn't. Ron was one of those guys who liked people shooting straight with him, and he certainly wouldn't hold back in conversation.

What was amazing was that there were so many things about God that Ron liked. He liked the idea of joy. He liked the idea of peace. He liked the idea of self-control (at least when it came to his career—not so much with the ladies). He was attracted to the goodness of God, but he was more than a little wary of finding the way to God.

He loved the bass line, but he was skeptical of the lyrics. He didn't want to dance until he could trust the whole song.

So one time I said, "Ron, a time will come when the things you love about God—the things that seem clear to you—will earn God enough trust with you so you can begin moving into the things that are unclear. But the unseen can't be seen until you begin moving into the spaces that you already see."

Put another way: sometimes we want to wait until we can hear the whole song before we start dancing. But it's in the act of engaging with the few elements of the music that we *can* hear that we begin to connect with the more complex melody we haven't yet heard. It's the dancing that helps us hear the full song.

The good news is that the music is always playing. And every one of us can hear at least parts of the song.

It's time to dance.

ELEVEN

Use What You Got

////////

On lists, LEGOs, quirks, and quarks

In 1932 a carpenter in the town of Billund, Denmark, founded a company to produce small wooden blocks for children to play with. In the 1950s the company started making the blocks out of plastic and soon after, sales dwindled. No one, they were told, wanted to play with plastic blocks.[1]

Of course, more than sixty years after the switch to plastic, the company makes six hundred blocks every second. The company name is LEGO.

My nephew Xander loves LEGOs. When he was five, it was impossible to have a conversation with him without his asking you to be on his LEGO team. The first time he asked, it was flattering. But later I realized that he asked *everybody*.

Even now, when I visit my sister (Xander's mom), he is usually in the zone—the LEGO zone. He's down on the floor near a coffee table that is covered with LEGOs. His little figures move in sync with his developing imagination. There's a kind of nirvana-esque calm about him as he builds little worlds. He keeps moving pieces around, seeing what works and what doesn't. His head is bowed like he's praying, and in many ways he is. He is creating, and creativity is always an act of faith.

Xander builds cars, houses, spaceships, towns, and lots of Star Wars set pieces. LEGOs are as low-tech as a phenomenal toy can be. They're simply interlocking pieces of plastic—a tactile way to express your creativity.

Sometimes when I watch my nephew at play I get a little nostalgic. Those were the good ol' days, I think, when it was possible to play all day and build whatever a kid wanted.

But then I think, how is my life today any different?

I get to play all day and build whatever I want. In fact, the older I get, the better the stuff is that I get to build. The same is true for many of my friends. Xander builds little toy cars, but I have friends who design concept cars for Honda. Young girls play house, but as adults we get to make families. Kids play in their own little worlds, yet as we grow older we discover we can create new worlds.

One Christmas I bought a nice little LEGO set for Xander. I was excited to give it to him on Christmas Day. That morning, after everyone had some of my dad's famous cinnamon biscuits, we all gathered 'round the tree to exchange gifts.

Xander is going to love my present, I told myself. I sat back and waited for the right time to give it to him.

And then I saw it: my parents, smiling at each other, picked up a giant box with a tag that read, "From Mimi and Papa to Xander." As soon as I saw the box, I knew what was inside. And my stomach dropped.

Xander's eyes got as big as salad plates as he ripped off the wrapping paper. It was the newest, biggest, coolest Star Wars LEGO set on the market. As Xander excitedly ran around the house, my parents beamed with pride. I looked down at my little box, pathetically wrapped. This was going to be a little anticlimactic.

Well, I thought, *might as well get this over with.*

Once my nephew had come back down to earth, I handed him the stupid present I had brought. Xander quickly opened it. There was a pause. And then...

"MORE LEGOs!"

The windows shattered from the pitch of his voice. Heaven came to earth. There *was* a God.

In that moment I was reminded that you can *never* have too many LEGOs. You can, on the other hand, have too many iPads. You can have too many cars. You can have too many houses.

But you can never have too many LEGOs. This is because LEGOs aren't just toys—they're tools. They're not something you simply use; they're something you use to create. They're a plastic means to a creative end.

When you look at all your LEGOs, your mind explodes with all the things you can do with them. All the things you can build. All the possibilities.

When you look at a showroom full of classic cars you have, well, a room full of cars. Good for you. You've successfully created a museum.

But a room full of LEGOs? You can build whatever you want.

As we grow older, our creativity has a chance to expand. We have more options, more ideas, more resources to draw on, and more life experience and wisdom to inform our creativity. We get, in a manner of speaking, more LEGOs to play with. And there always are more LEGOs to play with.

You see, risk requires you to use what you already have to get what you don't currently have. It requires you to be who you already are so you can become the person you never thought you could be.

Years ago I was driving home from Colorado with a college friend. The two of us had been in a wedding in Denver, and we had a long drive ahead of us. You should know that this friend was a special person, the type of girl that every guy at my college wanted to date. She was bubbly, she turned a lot of heads, and she was a very kind person. We were talking about whether she was going to start volunteering with a nonprofit in Kansas City, where she could work with girls in junior high school.

"I just don't feel like I have anything to offer," she said.

I looked at her in disbelief. "Let me get this straight: you have your college degree, you survived the last twenty-two years of life, you've worked through a lot of family issues, you've struggled through relationships and have made your own journey with God."

She said, "Yeah."

"And you're telling me there's not a single thing you know about life that a thirteen-year-old girl doesn't know? There's nothing you've learned that could help that girl—that could prevent her from making some of the same mistakes you did? You don't have a listening ear to offer, a kind shoulder to cry on, or a night to take these girls to the movies or have them over to talk and eat cookie dough?"

She smiled, realizing she had more to offer than she had imagined.

It's easy to be put off by the things we don't have or don't know. All the things that we're *not* can be overwhelming. Go ahead and fill in the blank: "I'm not _____."

Tall enough.

Smart enough.

Pretty enough.

Talented enough.

Experienced enough.

Kind enough.

Old enough.

We focus so much on what we're not that we easily forget everything that we are. But we should never allow the ocean of what we don't know to stop us from using the mountain of what we do know.

We are born with a lot of LEGOs. Then we accumulate more as we live and interact with others, and as we learn from God. Our personalities, strengths, quirks, interests, possessions, jobs, friends, and families all present us with opportunities to create something beautiful.

When Quirks Become Quarks

For six years I worked with students at Loyola Marymount University. We created a weekly campus event that facilitated dialogue on what it meant to be an inspiring human being. We called the event Late Night—mostly because it started at 10 p.m. every Tuesday night. (No creativity was wasted on the name.)

Over six years we brought in the most amazing, most inspiring people we could find. Grammy-winning artists, engineers from NASA, authors, spiritual gurus, leadership consultants. Each event featured original music and art from the student body, a fifteen-minute talk from the speaker, and then a Q&A.

It was some of the most fun I've ever had.

One of the most popular speakers was a man you've probably never heard of. His name is William Fulco, but everyone called him "Father." He is a priest.

Father Fulco is a genius. He's traveled the world. He speaks and understands twelve or so languages. He was the linguistic expert on Mel Gibson's *The Passion of the Christ.*

Father Fulco doesn't care about popularity. A man truly marked by grace, he speaks with humility and passion about his struggle with alcoholism. Every time he came to speak at Loyola Marymount, the venue would be packed. He expressed a sense of compassion for the frat boys present in the room, many of whom were already following the same trajectory he had been on at that age.

Once, when he was meeting with a much smaller group, Father Fulco's wisdom changed my life. Speaking to a few students, he said, "Write down everything you don't like about yourself: your looks, your quirks, your flaws. Anything about you that you wish you could change."

I don't know what I expected him to say next. Maybe "and now pray that God would remove those things from your life." Or maybe "God loves you in spite of those things."

Instead, he said, "Thank God for those things, for in them is a unique way for you to love others that no one else can duplicate."

If we had no flaws, quirks, or idiosyncrasies, we would be limited in the way we can love other people. Or put another way: our quirks are actually quarks. (Nerd alert: Quarks are some of the smallest building blocks of the universe. Atoms are made of quarks.) Your life and mine—every aspect of life—is a huge box of LEGOs. Even the things we don't like about ourselves, in God's eyes, are LEGOs. They are tools and building blocks that God will use to make something beautiful.

I saw Arnold Schwarzenegger, the action hero turned governor turned action hero, give the commencement address to the graduating class at USC a few years ago. His speech was titled "The Seven Secrets to My Success." Secret No. 1 was marrying a Kennedy. (It was a lot funnier back then, before the divorce.)

He explained that his personal traits—the things people pointed to as evidence that he would never amount to anything—were the same qualities he managed to turn into resources that helped build his success.

When he moved to America everyone told him, "You'll never be a movie star. No one can understand you." He spent years taking lessons to minimize his accent, but nothing worked. His thick Austrian accent remained.

So he decided to look for roles in movies where there wasn't a lot of dialogue or—more important—where the dialogue was short, quippy, and (in light of his crazy vocal inflection) unforgettable. Action movies were tailor-made for this guy.

"I'll be back."

"Come with me if you want to live."

"Get down!"

"It's not a tumor."

These phrases would not be staples of pop culture if they had been said originally by Bruce Willis or Tom Cruise. Arnold became a star because he made use of the things people pointed to as obstacles that would prevent him from succeeding. His quirk achieved his quest.

Arnold knew how to use his LEGOs. What are your LEGOs?

The Creative Life

It's impossible for humans to not create. Think you're not creative? Okay, try not creating.

When I worked with youth in Kansas City, one young woman in our program was blind and autistic. Her father had died, and the girl's mother—one of the bravest women I'd ever met—had brought her daughter to our organization hoping to get her into a positive environment. Abigail went on trips with the group; she hiked mountains and went camping with us.

One time at a summer camp, the leaders from the Kansas City group were talking with leaders from other groups. The other leaders commented on how well our students got along with one another. They also were impressed by how everyone rallied around Abigail to help her join in and fit in. Teenage guys took turns walking Abigail to different classes and activities. Teenage girls helped Abigail get dressed and even helped her use the rest room.

We explained that Abigail's gift to us was her condition. Her "problems" called us to greater acts of humility and servanthood.

Many people would look at a blind, autistic child and wrongly conclude that she's incapable of being creative. In fact, Abigail loved creating music. But Abigail's creativity went even further than that. Abigail created a strong community around her precisely because of her condition, not in spite of it. Abigail showed me that our lives—even including our dysfunction—are gifts to those around us. This is because our dysfunction is an opportunity for others to love when it is difficult.

Humans are constantly creating something. Right now I am creating carbon dioxide as I exhale. I'm also creating these words as I pound them out, letter by letter, on my computer keyboard.

We create when we act, because doing something creates movement. We also create when we don't act, because refusing to do something creates a vacuum.

And by the very fact of your existence, you are creating opportunities for other people to react to you. By living, we create opportunities for friends to love us, for enemies to oppose us, for our parents to wonder about us, and for the government to check up on us.

I created all this simply by deciding to get out of bed this morning and go out into the world. So did you. And consider how this effect is multiplied throughout the day by the words you will speak, the actions you'll take, the joy you bring, and the burdens you share with others.

Today you may tell a joke or offer a listening ear. Today you may give someone a hug or a handshake or a nudge. You may love the things you create, even if they are nothing more than a spreadsheet, a meeting agenda, dinner, or plans for a birthday party. Or you might hate what you create—tension in a room, a broken friendship, or a consumer product you're not proud of.

While you're reading this, you are creating new ideas. Maybe you're developing arguments to counter what I'm writing, or maybe your mind is wandering to a different place, where you're making a list of what you should be doing rather than reading a book.

All that you do constitutes a creative act in one form or another.

You can't deny it: you are a creator.

So if you can't help but be creative, you might as well be intentional about what you create and how you go about it. You might as well live life on your toes.

What do you expect from yourself? Don't strive to be perfect, but at least strive to be profound. Don't strive to be God, but at least strive to present a clearer image of God. Expect extraordinary things from yourself. Create extraordinary experiences for others.

TWELVE

The Secret Life of God

//////////

*Also known as "Take
your kid to work day"*

When I was a kid, I fell in love with a book called *Redwall* by Brian
Jacques. I'll never forget the first time I held the book in my hands
and saw on the cover a little mouse wearing an oversized dark-green
habit (similar to a monk's hooded robe). The mouse also was wearing clumsy, wooden flip-flops and was smiling triumphantly while
holding a sword. Nearby were vicious warrior rats holding daggers
and skulls.

It was clear the villains were going after the little mouse.

I was captivated.

Over the next few years I read that book at least a dozen times. I
couldn't resist the characters, the conflict, the adventure. Redwall
mythology spoke directly to me. Even as a kid, I longed to do something meaningful with my life. But I also felt small and clumsy like the
mouse on the book's cover. To my delight, over the course of the next
few years, Brian Jacques wrote at least a dozen more books expanding the Redwall universe. Prequels, sequels, in-between-quels. All

told, he created more than twenty Redwall books, which sold over 20 million copies worldwide and were translated into more than twenty languages. When the library would hold a book fair, I'd run to see if a new Redwall title had come out. This series was the best, and I'll arm-wrestle anyone who disagrees.

At the same time I was devouring Redwall books, I had one of the best teachers ever. Mrs. Butler was like a hippie-beatnik poet. She was Greek (I think), and she would always wear a black turtleneck. She was also very thin (like me) with a wide, black Afro (not like me). She was smart, creative, witty, and besides all that (or perhaps because of it), she was an excellent teacher.

She also knew of my love for the Redwall series.

One day after class she asked to speak with me. This was usually not good, but I remember having so much respect for Mrs. Butler that I wasn't nervous. "Jason," she said, "I spoke with your parents, and they gave me permission to ask you a question. Brian Jacques is going to do a book reading at the Reading Reptile in Westport, and my husband and I would like to have you over for dinner. Then we would take you to meet him and get one of your Redwall books signed."

Of course I was excited, but something didn't seem right. Packed in the paragraph above is a lot of information that just doesn't occur to an eleven-year-old boy:

Mrs. Butler is married?

Mrs. Butler has an apartment?

Mrs. Butler eats dinner?

I don't know if it was this way for you, but I rarely thought of my teachers as having, you know, lives outside of teaching us. I kind of just thought that after we left school at three o'clock, they went into teacher containers to recharge or something, like robots. So when Mrs. Butler invited me to have dinner with her husband in her cool West Plaza apartment, I was a little confused.

Come to think of it, I shouldn't have been all that confused. After all, my parents were teachers. Yet I'd seen a similar reaction on other kids' faces when I would go to the grocery store with one of my parents. One of my dad's students would walk up to him in the produce section and nervously say, "Hey, Mr. Jaggard."

What they were thinking was something like this: *What in the world are you doing here buying lettuce? Shouldn't you be grading papers or figuring out how to make our lives miserable or something? And who is this young child with you? Teachers don't have families.*

When we see people in one specific arena, it's easy to believe that who they are in that arena is all that they are. But Mrs. Butler wasn't a teacher only. She was also a wife, her husband was a great cook, they had a cool apartment, and she had beads hanging in her doorway.

I experienced this in reverse with my parents, whom I thought of as parents first and foremost. But then I'd have a chance to see them at work. At first it was weird to see my dad interact with high school students or to see my mom teach music. But then I got to discover how amazing they are at teaching.

My dad won an award for excellence in education, and they flew our family to Washington, DC, for the ceremony. In the classroom he is funny, confident, and inspiring.

Then there's my mom. Kids love my mom. For thirty years she taught elementary school music. To this day former students still come up to her and give her hugs. "Hey, Mrs. Jaggard!" they shout, smiling ear to ear.

My parents were actually cool, in a teacher sort of way.

Here's the point of all this. The more I saw my parents at work, the more I understood who they were. I didn't see them solely as adults who loved me and read me bedtime stories and forced me to do the dishes. I realized there were whole worlds outside of my life that they were involved in and that they cared about deeply. There were sides of them I didn't get to see until I went to work with them. And now that I'm a teacher at the college level, I understand my parents in a whole new way.

Jesus once said, "My Father is always at his work." Another time He said, "The Son...can do only what he sees his Father doing."[1]

Recently I've begun thinking of Jesus's life as a kind of take-your-son-to-work program. Jesus understood God in ways that others couldn't because He got to see sides of God that others didn't see. He got to experience God because He went to work with God.

When we don't participate in what God is doing in the world, He can become blurry and indecipherable. Perhaps it is rare that we experience God...simply because we haven't bothered to go to work with Him. It stands to reason that there are whole other parts of His personality that we have yet to discover or understand because we have not seen Him in action.

The Blurry God

Ever notice how things, when they move really fast, become blurry? If you were to wave your hand in front of your face right now, it would be a blur. Or look at a ceiling fan that's spinning. You won't see five individual blades; you'll just see a blur of motion.

Your mind can process only about thirty separate images per second. So anything that moves faster than that looks like a blur. And when something is blurred, you can't see the details.

If you want to get a clear look at a car that is racing around a track at 190 miles per hour, the thing to do is to drive at 190 miles per hour alongside it. The best view of a NASCAR race is enjoyed by the drivers. It's not just because of proximity, but also because of trajectory. They get a long look at the cars around them.

And here is how your view of God compares to watching a NASCAR race. When God moves and you stand still, God becomes blurry. Oftentimes the only way to see God clearly is to move along with Him. If you feel God has been absent, maybe it's because He's on the move and you're still sitting in the stands.

You start seeing God more clearly when you step into a moment of risk. Taking a risk has a way of capturing your attention and making you more aware of what is going on around you. Taking a risk reminds you of all the ways you feel incomplete, ill-equipped, and generally unprepared. Following God is a risky move, and He looks different when you're following Him. Things change when you live intentionally, setting your agenda according to God and His plans for humanity.

This explains why so many people who would say they're searching for God are often closer to Him than those who feel they have already found Him. People who search are on the move. And sadly, once people find God, they tend to stop moving.

On Being (Re)born

My sister's baby practically fell out of the womb. Trust me, if you think reading that is gross, then you should see the video. (Okay, we fast-forwarded through certain parts to avoid anything that could be considered unnatural.) Being born is a messy deal. There is nothing romantic about it.

But as I watched my nephew enter the world, the strangest thing happened. There was all this gross, yucky stuff happening, and suddenly I saw Anthony—my brother-in-law—crying. "He's so beautiful," Anthony kept saying in between sobs. Where I saw blood and fluids, my brother-in-law saw his son. He saw beauty, life, and meaning.

Birth isn't an inherently beautiful thing unless you know what to look for.

Birth is, I'm assuming, embarrassing for the baby. Think about it: You come sailing out naked and bloody and gross. You don't have skinny jeans or matching Gap apparel. It's just you and slimy watery stuff. Somebody slaps you, they take away your familiar food source with scissors (and if you're a boy, they take away even more), and then you're off to be measured and such. You don't really know a whole lot about what's going on. But one thing you know for sure: you're alive and your world just got a whole lot bigger.

There's an ancient story about Jesus meeting a Jewish scholar named Nicodemus. Nicodemus was confused. He'd been a religious leader his whole life, but he didn't understand what Jesus was doing or saying. So he approached Jesus in the middle of the night to get some answers. During the conversation, Jesus told Nick that he had to be reborn if he wanted to understand God and what on earth was going on.

Nick was a grown man and a respected figure in Jerusalem. He didn't warm to Jesus's idea. After all, entering into a mother's womb and then coming out again is not that sexy of a proposition, as we well know. Plus, Nicodemus could picture the logistical problems. He realized that neither the mother nor the adult son would enjoy such an experience.

So Jesus said, "No. You're not getting it. Unless you are born of the Spirit, you cannot experience the kingdom of God." When speaking of being "born of the Spirit," Jesus used the phrase "born again."[2]

I've heard this expression most of my life and, to be honest, I've never liked it all that much. It makes me think of televangelists with big rings and abundant hair, Jimmy Carter, and sociology statistics. People sometimes ask me, "Are you a 'born again' Christian?" I didn't know there was any other kind.

To Jesus, being reborn didn't mean you held a particular set of doctrinal beliefs or that you adhered to certain lifestyle restrictions. It didn't mean you were pro-life or that you attended a certain style of church or that you were anti-Disney. To be reborn means that your spirit has met God, and God has told your spirit that it has been in the womb for too long. It's time to be free. It's time to humble yourself and to be born a second time—which means you enter a new life in which you start moving with the Spirit of God. It will be risky. It will be messy. It will be humbling. It will be a mystical mystery.

But it's the only way to see the kingdom of God. And the view is breathtaking.

Being reborn is entering into the big picture. It's discovering the heart and mission of God and connecting to both. It's leaving the womb of your little self and partnering with a God who has a thing for humanity and is doing something about it.

Being reborn means living a life of risk. The writer of the book of James seems pretty intent on making this clear when he writes that faith that is free of risk is lifeless. He later writes that when we don't take the risks we know we ought to take, it's actually destructive not only to our own souls but to the souls of those we're connected to.[3]

Referring to the ancient stories of the Hebrew scriptures, James wrote that Abraham was justified because of his risk. His life proved his faith. James's writing assures us that risk and faith are intertwined, and one without the other is worthless.[4] Divine faith always involves risk.

So being reborn—living a life of risk—is like the moment in the movie *Ocean's Eleven* when George Clooney looks at Matt Damon, with airline tickets to the adventure of his life lying on the table, and says: "You're either in or you're out. Right now."[5]

Next scene: There's our boy, Matt. He's a rookie, sure, but he took the ticket. And now he's propelled into the drama of *Ocean's Eleven*.

That's God's dream for the life of every person: to propel us into an adventure that will exceed anything we could imagine. In fact, the question Jesus asked Nicodemus bears more than a passing similarity to Clooney's challenging Damon. Except Jesus, rather than asking "Are you in or out?" was saying, "Are you out or in? Are you out of the womb, reborn? Or are you in the womb, wasting time?"[6]

God wants to propel you into His great drama of faith, love, and hope. God wants to give you Life. He wants to overhaul your heart and unleash your soul to serve the world on His behalf.

And risk is your ticket to ride.

Maybe so many people who claim the name Christian are bored out of their minds because they're still waiting around in the womb. They're one-hundred-plus-pound babies who never were reborn; they never stepped out into the light of day.

Maybe the greatest indictment of organized Christianity is that churches produce remade people but not reborn people. Has your spirit been reborn? Have you entered into the current of God's wind? Can you feel the Spirit moving through our dying world? Are you moving with Him?

Now is your chance. It will be risky. It will be messy. It will be humbling. Others may look at you and think you're crazy. But just as my newborn nephew brought tears of joy to his dad's eyes, you will be beautiful in the sight of God.

So are you in or out? Or should I ask, "Are you out or in?"

THIRTEEN

Community on the Go

//////////

The gospel according to Ocean's Eleven

The great poet-philosopher Dane Cook once said that every man has two overarching desires:

1. To own a pet monkey.
2. To go on a heist.

The monkey part is obvious. I mean, c'mon. Monkeys are just awesome.

But a heist is *even better.* I know, because some of the best movies to come out of Hollywood are heist films. Here are a few classics:

The Sting.

Heat.

Inception.

The Usual Suspects.

Mission: Impossible.

And, of course, *Ocean's Eleven.*

The best heist films involve a group of highly gifted people who come together to pull off the impossible and have a ball doing it. That description also applies to my favorite definition of community. Community isn't simply a network of relationships. It's not just about friends or family. Community at its finest is *up to something.* It's on a mission.

Community is on the go, and very likely it involves people coming together to pull off the impossible and have a ball doing it.

Remove the action from community at your own peril. Ever had a relationship stagnate and die? Ever been part of a dysfunctional family, church, company, or any other relational network? Dysfunction often grows out of having no shared goal. No purpose. No healthy drama. No heist. Our souls *long* for drama, and when there is no healthy cause to invest in, the drama deteriorates into melodrama.

You get gossip, slander, who did what to whom. When we aren't engaged in healthy, creative movement forward, we'll naturally start to make some trouble in order to fill the void in our lives.

There's a classic scene from *Ocean's Twelve,* the worthy sequel to *Ocean's Eleven,* where Danny Ocean and Rusty Ryan are in Germany talking about the state of their lives after having given up thieving.

"It sucks," Danny says.

He continues. "I don't know. Can't turn my brain off, you know. It's me. We go into some place, and all I can do is see the angles. It's what I do. It's what I've always done. I love it."[1]

Danny is talking about the longing inside all of us. The longing to be part of something exciting, something fun, something that is meaningful to us and that is carried out together with people we trust.

Whether it's Robert Redford and Paul Newman in *The Sting* or George Clooney and Brad Pitt in *Ocean's Eleven,* there is something smart, exciting, and just plain fun about people doing something risky in a way that allows each one to play an important role.

It's fun to watch on the screen, but it's even *more* fun when we get to do it ourselves.

Life as a Heist

When we created Late Night, the weekly event at Loyola Marymount University, we didn't know what we were doing or even if it was going to work. All we knew was that we wanted to create an environment where students could interact with the question, What does it look like to be an inspiring human being?

While success was uncertain, I knew one thing for sure: the team of people that came together to pull this off every week was unbelievable. There was Alex. She was and still is one of the most administratively gifted people I've ever met. She was not only able to keep us on course and organized, but she was also able to sense when people were hurting or needed encouragement. Full of hospitality, Alex was kind of like the mom of Late Night.

Then there was Ryan (whom we affectionately called Happy). Ryan was a constant source of positive energy. As a water polo player, he stood six feet, four inches tall and had the body of a bronzed god (not so much anymore). Ryan could turn any gathering into a party. His mischievous spirit made Late Night a lot of fun.

We had Rosie (who has since gone on to play Olympic water polo on Canada's national team). Talented, passionate, and fearless. Her zeal for what we were doing often would keep us going. She was the keeper of the flame, the leader whose integrity and inner beauty often made Late Night what it was.

We had Jomar, who worked part-time for the university. He is an incredible musician and is one of the most sincere folks you'll ever meet. He made sure that every Late Night event had musical talent to inspire and entertain the students who came. Jomar also had connections with the fraternities on campus, which gave us some credibility in those circles.

And Sean, who was the good-natured, "jump in wherever" guy. His smile lit up a room. Jomar, Rosie, Ryan, and Sean also all had amazing musical talent. They still perform at various venues today, from nightclubs to coffee shops.

Last but not least was June. We all refer to June as the Godmother. She worked full-time at the university and helped us pull strings to get what we needed (space, lights, sound). June was the one who introduced me to Rosie and Ryan, and she's the one who thought that maybe something special could happen if we worked together.

These people were incredible on their own. But when they came together, they couldn't be stopped. Together they created energy; no, more than that. They created *synergy* that made people feel welcomed and inspired.

It was beautiful.

A ragtag group of twenty-year-olds created an environment every week where fifty to one hundred of their friends could talk about things that mattered. They did this with practically zero budget and little support from older adults.

Helping them out was some of the most fun I've ever had. Every week was like pulling off a heist. But instead of stealing something, we were *giving* something. We were giving people permission to be extraordinary. We were giving people challenges to make beautiful choices. We were giving people reminders of their inherent worth and inviting them to become stewards of the one and only life that God had given them.

This fulfills a deep longing in our souls: to partner with others to pull off the meaningful and have a ball doing it.

The same type of thing happens on a smaller scale when people spark with others. During a Spark Group in Whittier, California, one person discovered that a restaurant in uptown Whittier was struggling to make it. One person with little to no money can't save a restaurant. But *fifteen* people could make a bigger impact. So for a few weeks, the group had dinner at the struggling restaurant on its slowest night to help with sales, and then they spread the word about the great food and quality service.

Years later, the restaurant is still in business and everyone from that initial Spark Group gets a fifteen-percent discount. Not bad.

If only one person had risked helping out that restaurant, it wouldn't have done much. There'd be good intentions, sure. There'd even be good action, but little impact. In that case the action had to be bigger.

Make. It. Bigger.

Honestly, my natural inclination is to think small. When I think of a risk, I tend to think in terms of just me: what I can do. Nothing wrong with this. It's a great place to start. It's just a horrible place to finish.

So I've found a simple trick that I use to develop dreams that are a little more challenging. It involves just three words:

Make. It. Bigger.

To make something bigger, you have to start with something. So the first step is to make something happen, even if it's small. Here's an example. Let's say you'd like to volunteer, maybe go to a school once a week and read to an underprivileged child. That's fantastic. In fact, *go and do that.* Do it for a few months. That might be a big enough risk for you at first, and it's a great way to get things started.

One of my early sparks was volunteering for Meals On Wheels (Mowaa.org), an organization that delivers fresh meals to elderly folks. My grandfather had volunteered for Meals On Wheels for decades in the Midwest. At the time I got involved, he could no longer volunteer after having had a stroke. I decided to volunteer out here in California. My plan was to give my grandfather a call in Kansas while I was on my route, and it'd give us something to talk about.

When I checked with Meals On Wheels to see if I could start delivering meals, I was nervous. Volunteering is a small thing, but it wasn't in my routine. I had never been involved with this organization, and the elderly can be a little intimidating. *What if they don't like me, can't hear me, or think I'm a mugger?*

I imagine you are as tired of reading my excuses as I am of writing them.

The first week they partnered me with Joyce, a sixty-year-old woman who loved three things: riding motorcycles, talking, and smoking. I reminded her later that two of her hobbies would probably make her a recipient of Meals On Wheels someday. Either way, she knew what she was doing, so I was glad to be with her.

They gave us a route. We picked up warm meals and sack lunches, loaded the food in my trunk, and we were off. I had no idea what was in store.

As we pulled up to the first house, Joyce looked at me with a wry smile and said, "The first drop is Shirley. How about you take this one?"

How very nice of her, I thought. I nervously grabbed the designated food and walked up to the house; then I timidly knocked on the door.

No answer. I knocked louder.

"I'M NAKED!" came the response.

Well, okay then.

I waited for a minute. Suddenly the door snapped open as far as the chain lock would allow. I could see a bright blue eye suspiciously scanning me through the crack. Fortunately, Shirley had put on a muumuu.

"Uh...I'm with Meals On Wheels," I said.

One white eyebrow lifted with surprise, and then Shirley happily said, "Oh, well, come in! Come in!"

The door slammed shut, the chain unlocked, and the door opened to show Shirley: a short, white-haired woman with sky-blue eyes and a matching muumuu with a lace collar.

"Hello, Shirley," I said. "That's a very nice dress you have on."

She blushed and said, "Oh, honey, I'm a diabetic. You keep talking like that and I'm going to go into insulin shock!"

That was the beginning of my friendship with Shirley. Over the next few months, I would learn a little about her family and her life, and occasionally I'd put the tennis ball back on one of the legs of her walker. And Meals On Wheels became something I looked forward to. But my contribution wasn't, you know, big.

This is where our risks often end. We have an idea, and then we take a risk and volunteer. It goes well; we get comfortable; it's a successful mission. And we think that's as good as things can get. That is the perfect time to *make it bigger.*

Let's say you've been volunteering at a school, where you read to a child. To make it bigger, you could expand the effort so that five kids will have someone reading to them. Or it could grow to fifty kids—or a hundred.

You might be thinking, *I don't have that kind of time.* You'd be right. That's why you'd need to include other volunteers.

With Spark Groups a woman named Mandy faced just that sort of challenge. She had asked her five-year-old son what kind of risk he'd like to make in order to make himself a better person or the world a better place. After thinking about it, he said, "I know there are kids without backpacks and school supplies in Los Angeles. We should do something about that."

Initially, Mandy and her family thought they'd donate one backpack and that would be a great little risk for a five-year-old. But she found out that "they don't really accept just one backpack as a donation."

So her family decided to make it bigger. The four of them decided to donate fifty backpacks. But in order to do that, they needed to partner with someone else. Their faith community graciously took up the banner.

Mandy's son made a flier, and pastors in the community let him give an announcement before church gatherings.

At first there was little response. Only a few backpacks came in. But after a few weeks, they had ten, then twenty, then forty. They didn't know if they were going to meet their goal of fifty, but by the end of the backpack drive, the family, in partnership with their faith community, had collected more than one hundred fifty backpacks—a giant pile of them.

How did one five-year-old kid do so much? Simple. He made it bigger.

Make the goal big enough, and you will have to ask others for help. Make it inspiring enough, and most of the time people will be glad to help out.

Here's another story, this one from outside of Chicago. A man named George had been visiting his mom at a nursing home. One of her favorite residents was an older man who loved ice cream. By the time George's Spark Group had gotten underway, the man at the nursing home had passed away. So George decided to buy ice cream for every resident of the nursing home, in honor of his mom's friend.

Thing is, George couldn't afford to buy that much ice cream. He had to recruit others to join in.

As I was hearing his story, I thought: *Who* wouldn't *want to buy ice cream for a nursing home! How fun is* that?

George successfully recruited a team to help him accomplish a beautiful goal. It made his mom's day. The nursing home residents still talk about it.

These are all heists. But instead of robbing casinos, we're saving restaurants. Instead of stealing drugs, we're giving backpacks. Instead of conning the bad guy, we're giving away ice cream to the elderly.

Same muscles, really. Just a different aim.

For my spark with Meals On Wheels, I decided I wasn't going to volunteer alone. I sent out some e-mails and texted a few friends and, pretty soon, I began taking friends with me to volunteer. We'd get to talk in the car, we'd do something meaningful, and they'd get to meet Shirley.

What I love about inviting others into what you're doing is that it's not just about you and your dream. When we recruit others into what we're doing, we're inviting them into enjoying the thrill of doing something meaningful and fun. In fact, the more you enjoy your life, the more important it is to bring others into it.

When Models Aren't Enough

A few weeks ago I was hanging out with a friend in the Arts District in downtown Los Angeles. He is an incredible human being. Ryan is one of those rare combinations of humility and power. He likes nice things—he flew to Germany to buy a brand-new BMW M3, cruised around Europe for a few days, and then shipped the car home. Yet Ryan is also one of the most genuine and caring people I know.

While we were hanging out, he was sharing an incredible experience he'd had the day before while listening to God. Ryan couldn't say enough about how much he was enjoying this season of life.

I'd like to say that I was happy for him. I guess I was, or part of me was. But I'll be honest: most of me was jealous that he was having such a beautiful experience with God and I wasn't. His story was meant to inspire me, but it just made me grumpy.

Later that night I confessed to him how I felt. It wasn't his fault, but listening to him talk about how great his spiritual life was going was not having the intended effect on me. What ensued was a great conversation about leadership. Ryan asked, "Jason, what could I have done that would have helped you with your jealousy?"

Of course, it wasn't Ryan's responsibility to help me with my jealousy, but I appreciated his asking. "That's easy," I said. "Invite me to have the same experience *with* you."

If all you do is model—if you only take beautiful risks on your own—you run the risk of creating a chasm between you and other people. Either people will elevate you as some sort of superhuman who does what they're not capable of, or they call you to mind as a reminder of their own inadequacies. It can be a lose-lose situation. Either they idolize you or resent you. Or sometimes both.

I suppose one possible solution is to pretend that your life *isn't* awesome. Or to not share your love, joy, and exuberance for life with others. But there is a far better option: *invite* others to come with you. God rarely calls us into an adventure that can be pulled off by just one person. You can't become who you were meant to become without the help of others.

Beckoning others to come with you is recognition that you're enjoying life and that you long for others to share in the same experience. It's not enough to model a new life; we have to recruit.

Coincidentally, one of my personal Sparks was to do something really nice for Ryan. He volunteers much of his time for our company. When Spark Good was first getting off the ground, Ryan would pay for his own flight so that he could travel with me and we could work together.

I wanted to say "thank you" in a way that would really mean something to him. I wanted to do something special, but I'm a horrible gift giver. So I got the idea to ask his brother what my friend might like.

I called his brother, who lives in San Diego, and had a wonderful conversation with him. You would think that it might have been a little awkward, since I was calling essentially for intel on his brother, but it wasn't. He was now part of the kindness conspiracy. He had been recruited.

He gave me some great ideas for something nice I could do for his brother. I added a few personal touches and then gave one of the most thoughtful gifts I had ever put together.

What is it that you want to see happen in your life, or in the life of someone else, that can't happen unless you recruit others to help? People are our greatest resource, and most of the time they are happy to help when we ask.

So any time someone asks you a question and your answer is, "I don't know," it could be followed with, "But I know someone who does." That is, after you have practiced inviting others into your life adventures.

FOURTEEN

Life at the End
/////////// of Ourselves

*When what we've got is not
enough, and why that's okay*

My favorite moment of any film is Act 3, the final showdown. It's where all the things learned so far by the heroes will be put to the test. The driving question in Act 3 is, Will they be able to pull it off?

This is usually when my more excitable friends move to the front edge of their seats. They might even start bouncing.

It's Luke Skywalker going to blow up the Death Star in *Star Wars*.

It's Danny Ocean walking into the heavily defended casino that his gang is about to rob blind.

It's Billy Crystal (Harry) running through the streets of New York City on New Year's Eve to confess his undying love to Meg Ryan (Sally) in *When Harry Met Sally*.

In fact, when you see any man running toward any diner, plane, party, or taxi (usually in the rain) to catch the girl, you *know* you're in Act 3. This is the part of the story when everything is on the line. It's when the hero has done all he or she can do. All that remains is to see how Fate decides this movie will end.

Why are we so drawn to Act 3? Because it's the moment when the lead character has reached the end of herself. This is the moment of greatest effort and of greatest trust.

It's Neo jumping out of a helicopter toward Morpheus, who's jumping out of the window of a skyscraper—just before they catch each other midair in *The Matrix*.

It's Tarzan swinging on a vine—trusting for dear life that the vine won't break—as he reaches out for the next vine. He's swinging through the jungle, having the time of his life.

It's what happens when we've done everything that is humanly possible; we have exhausted our intelligence and cunning, and we realize it's still *not enough*. This is when we need something greater than ourselves to pull us through.

Act 3 touches us deeply, because it gets at one of the most raw and vulnerable of human conditions. It's oftentimes our moment of greatest failure. Or it can become our finest hour.

Unfortunately, many of us never experience the thrill of being finite. Until we arrive at this point, we will never understand that in order to become great, we will need the help of something greater than ourselves.

When I quit my job in Kansas City to move to Los Angeles, I had no idea what the future held. But I knew what I was leaving behind: a great job, a nice salary, my own office and administrative assistant (she was fantastic). My boss had created a custom-designed career path for me. And now I was walking away from it all. It frustrated him to no end.

My boss wasn't the only one who was frustrated. Many of my friends and colleagues told me they couldn't understand why I would leave a promising career to move to La La Land, home of yoga, health food, and NPR. The bottom line for me had nothing to do with geography or climate or excitement or testing the waters of the unknown. It was as simple as this: In the past few years I had realized that my life did not reflect who I wanted to be. I had no idea how to change that if I stayed where I was. I needed to make a change in location in order to pursue this other change I was drawn to.

I'd heard rumors about a spiritual community in Los Angeles called Mosaic, which placed a huge premium on character development and servant leadership. These were things I desperately wanted. So I packed up my new Toyota Corolla and drove twenty-four hours, alone, to a new land. I did what I could do in the hopes that God could shape me in ways I could not.

It was terrifying. At times it felt like a mistake. And it ranks among the three best decisions I've ever made. There have been moments since I moved to Los Angeles that I literally had to pinch myself. My life has changed in such powerful ways.

These have been by far the most excruciating years of my life...and yet I wouldn't trade them for anything.

It might sound crazy, but that's what happens when your life enters a phase where you are near the end of yourself. It stops becoming about living a life of comfort and shifts toward living a life of meaning.

But none of this can happen until you start jumping, even when you're afraid.

Jump When You're Afraid

My life as a speaker has been unconventional. I gave my first talk at a camp when I was a freshman in high school. It was an anxious, ten-minute, stand-up routine with some random points about life sprinkled here and there.

Afterward, some people came up and said, "Dude, you were *so* funny." The first few folks who said this made me feel great. After all, who doesn't want to be liked? But then I noticed a trend. "Funny" was the only feedback I was getting. They couldn't remember a single point I had made. (And frankly, neither could I.) They couldn't remember anything meaningful, other than I'd made them laugh. If I were a comedian (trust me, I'm not), that would be fine. But at that camp, I had wanted to say something important, something that would move my fellow campers into a better life.

As I got older, I knew that I enjoyed being in front of an audience. I love ideas and I love sharing ideas, so teaching and speaking were a natural fit for me. But here's the thing: every time, before I got up to speak, I got nervous.

I mean really, *really* nervous.

We're talking room-is-spinning, hyperventilating, throwing-up, wishing-I-could-pass-out nervous.

I would have panic attacks. It didn't matter what the venue was like, the nature of the gathering, or the mood of the audience. (However, the larger the audience, the more nervous I would get.) It was like an anxiety meter:

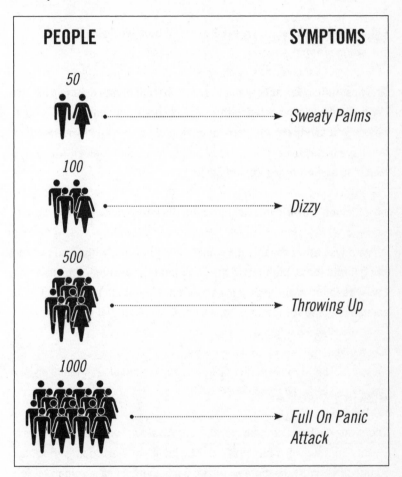

It is said that most people would rather die than speak in front of a large group. In the words of Jerry Seinfeld, "Most people would rather be the guy in the coffin than have to stand up and give a eulogy."[1]

For me it was a strange combination of both. I knew I wanted to speak, and I felt like I had something to say. My community affirmed that I was effective as a speaker, but still I was terrified every time I did it.

I guess you could say it was the worst of both worlds: I'd rather give the eulogy *from* the coffin.

The first time I was scheduled to speak in front of more than five hundred people, I came down with a case of "one-talk syndrome." That's where you are given only one opportunity to speak, so you feel like you have to say everything and say it perfectly and make it funny and touching and memorable and perfect.

My talk would be given at a church on Christmas Day. I freaked out.

A few days before the event, I went to my boss and, with hands trembling, I told him I couldn't do this. Fortunately, my boss's brother-in-law was in town and was a great communicator, so he stepped in at the last second.

Not a great start to a speaking career.

Risking Disaster

Years later, when I started working for Awaken, I was asked to give a twenty-minute introduction to the training we were doing that day. About one hundred people would be participating in a seminar. My job was to set up the concepts of positive psychology and introduce the main ideas behind Gallup's StrengthsFinder assessment. No big deal, right?

I prepared for three days *straight*.

The other day I was cleaning out some files and found my notes for this talk. There were pages and pages of thoughts, quotes, ideas, activities, points, and brainstorms. I had to smile. Now when I go to give a twenty-minute talk, I might take along a napkin with a few words scribbled on it. But for my first time teaching with Awaken, I wanted to deliver the Magna Carta.

The results were disastrous. I talked for an hour. It was long. It was rambling. It was like watching a four-year-old try to hold twenty marbles in his little clenched fist. The harder I clung to the marbles, the more they popped out and scattered across the floor.

Afterward, the woman leading the event said, "Jason, it was like you didn't spend time preparing at all. You can't just wing it, you know." I showed her my pages of notes. It wasn't that I hadn't prepared. It's that I had prepared *poorly.*

A few years after that I was asked to speak at Mosaic at a gathering of about a thousand people. I wish I could say my talk was a lights-out success. It wasn't.

I freaked out *again.* Had to cancel. My friend stepped in at the last second.

So fast-forward a little. I was asked to speak to a few college students at a university on the East Coast. I thought, *Address a class of students? No problem. I love the classroom environment.*

About a month before the event, I got a call from my friend who had set up the opportunity. "Hey, man," he said. "I have some news. You're not going to be speaking to a class."

I was a little bummed by the news, but nothing prepared me for what he said next.

"Instead, you'll be speaking to my entire university."

I got a lump in my throat. I was excited, sure. I was also terrified. But I thought, *This is a private school. Surely there couldn't be more than a thousand or so students.*

"No problem," I said. "How many students are there?"

He told me the number.

Now here's the thing about cell phones: sometimes you can't hear what is being said—especially when it's important. "I'm sorry," I said. "Could you repeat that? It sounded like you said ten *thousand*."

"That's what I said."

I almost fell over.

I've never tried so hard to get out of doing something. At Mosaic I was surrounded by speakers who were more experienced than I was. I made a list and approached them all. For me to be a good steward of this opportunity, I needed to give it to someone who would do a better job at it.

Looking back I'm a little embarrassed at how aggressively I wanted to avoid an opportunity to step into something incredible. I felt like a cockroach when the light is turned on in the kitchen, scrambling to hide someplace dark. I wanted the opportunity, but I was afraid that I wasn't capable.

This made me think, *I wonder how often I've missed opportunities without even knowing it? How often do I rob God of the joy of being God in my life?*

There's this tendency in many of us to just stay where it's safe—to avoid opportunities that would demand something from us that we're not sure we can give. And that, if anything, defines a life without God—a life that doesn't need Him to exist.

For me, it feels good to stay in the darkness rather than come out into the light. There is so much less pressure. So when I learned I'd be speaking in front of ten thousand students, it was settled in my mind. I'd find someone else to do it.

You can imagine my horror when every one of my friends declined my invitation to have them take my place. "This is *your* opportunity," they said.

Jerks.

Jumping into the Night

A month later the folks organizing my trip picked me up from the airport and drove me onto a beautiful college campus. I stared at the ten-story arena where I would address the student body the next day. I couldn't eat. I worked on my talk. I reworked it. I worked it over one more time. That night I hardly slept.

The following morning I walked into the arena to see four jumbo screens, each one several stories tall. The crew had multiple cameras set up.

The friend who had invited me walked up with some doughnuts. "Hungry?" he asked.

Not unless you want to see it again later.

"Oh, by the way. This is going to be televised," he said.

I excused myself and threw up.

It didn't stop there. Backstage, while waiting to go on, I threw up some more. Then I repeated the process during the music that led up to my time to speak. I felt bad for the friend who had invited me. The staff at the college had to have been thinking, *Is this guy going to make it? Whose idea was it to bring him in, anyway?*

As I walked onto the stage, my heart was saying, "This is it. A moment to say something that could possibly help someone." But my body was saying, "This is it. You are going to die."

In the first five minutes I almost passed out. I had to jump up and down a little just to keep my heart rate up. Thirty minutes later, I finished on time and nearly ran off stage.

As strange as it sounds, after it was over all I could think was, *Let's do that again!*

And then what happened next honestly shocked me. Scores of students came up afterward and wanted to connect. I met a young woman who was attending the university—it's a religious school—but she considered herself an agnostic. She said she had been touched by what I'd said, and we conversed several times via e-mail about her journey and her struggles with God. And she wasn't the only one. Many students called and e-mailed Mosaic, where I was working back in Los Angeles, inquiring about our community. My friend at the college told me that my talk became one of the year's favorites.

It was an amazing trip.

Sometimes we do things in spite of our fear. Other times we do things *because* of our fear. For me, I long to speak even though the journey from my mind to the stage is a fearful and painful one. But every time I do it, God seems to meet me there.

That's what happens when we risk: we experience God in a way we couldn't otherwise. When we risk, we jump into the night and into the arms of God, come what may. It doesn't always go the way we'd hoped, but it always goes in a way God can use to create hope.

On Beautiful Mistakes

Not long ago I had a growing desire to give a certain sum of money to a cause I believed in. The sum wouldn't be a huge amount to a lot of people, but it was a lot for me. I'm not a super generous guy, but I had just received a great work opportunity that allowed a gift like this to be given.

So the question in my mind was: Whom or what will I give the money to?

Now, I have a lot of friends doing amazing things in the world. My friend Tyler is CEO of Project 7 (Project7.com), a company that gives a large percentage of its income to seven areas of global need. Paul, another friend, does extensive work with World Vision (Worldvision. com), a nonprofit that provides health care, education, and spiritual support to orphans worldwide. And then there's Michael, who works with Generosity Water (Generositywater.org), an organization committed to ending water scarcity in developing countries.

There also are a few faith communities that I'm a huge fan of. They're doing beautiful things in Los Angeles.

So what to do? I prayed and listened.

I didn't hear anything.

I really wanted to give the money soon. I knew if I held on to it, I would begin to see it as part of my life rather than as a gift to be given away... like when I buy a book for someone else and read it first before giving it to them.

So I picked the organization I thought I wanted to give the money to. I went online, rocked the payment information, and clicked the Donate button.

Instantly, I felt a pang of regret. I realized which of the other causes I *really* wanted to give the money to.

Oftentimes when it comes to being generous, the question nags at us: *What if I picked the "wrong" cause or gave to the "wrong" charity?* After I made the donation, feelings of guilt and shame started to flood my heart. The spirituality of Jenga was alive and well. I felt as though I'd pulled out the wrong game piece and the whole structure was tilting.

Then I realized that through giving to the "wrong" organization, I had been given a gift. I now knew with certainty where I wanted to invest my resources the next time. In my desire to hear the voice of God, I was asking God to speak and He was asking me to *act*.

Sometimes God calls us to wait until He speaks. Other times He is waiting for us to act. And other times still, He won't speak *until* we act. It's in the acting that we hear Him speak. It's when we move that we begin to see God more clearly.

The Wrong Thing Done for the Right Reasons

There's an odd passage of scripture that tells the darker side of the Christmas story.[2] There's a young man who is in love. There's a beautiful teenage girl who is engaged to the young man. He imagines their life together, a life of affection and honor. They will create a family together.

One day the teenage girl looks worried. She tells the young man they need to talk. She begins to describe some scandalous, frankly incredible, realities. The story she tells is so unbelievable, and the shock is so great, that the young man picks up only bits and pieces.

Baby.

Pregnant.

Their future together is gone. His honor has been dirtied by a duplicitous fiancée. She won't admit to her unfaithfulness. She instead blames the whole thing on God. *God* made her pregnant, she insists. An angel told her so. The young man is tortured with visions of his lover's infidelity. *Who's the father? How can this be happening to me?*

Many men in that time would have grabbed their fiancée's arm, dragged her into the public courtyard, declared her shame to the world, and had her killed by stoning.

Not Joseph. He loved his fiancée, Mary. So he chose to take a huge risk. The scriptures say that because he was an honorable man, "he had in mind to divorce her *quietly*."[3] No spectacle. No shaming. By refusing to deal with his pregnant fiancée publicly, as the law allowed, he was sacrificing his urge to clear his name. He was moving forward with what he felt was the best possible option for both of them: a quiet divorce.

Then one night, with the divorce papers on his desk, he had a dream. An angel appeared. I can imagine Joseph, in the dream, wondering, *Why an angel? Maybe I was wrong about Mary.*

And the angel explains everything.

God has a wonderful way of stepping in when we do the wrong thing for the right reasons. Joseph's heart was set on doing the *honorable* thing. He thought the honorable thing was to privately, out of the public eye, divorce his pregnant fiancée. But God helped him discover that the best course of action was something entirely different. Something *better*.

Joseph was already taking action. He was in motion, doing the honorable thing to protect Mary. And after he was moving, God spoke to him.

I try to do a similar thing. I ask myself, *What is the most honorable thing I can do in this situation?* And then I listen to God *while* I move.

Hey, if God wants you to do something else, He knows where you live. He'll let you know, as long as you're paying attention.

In regard to my donating money to the "wrong" cause, I don't regret it at all. In fact, the biggest result of my giving (aside from the *actual* giving) was discovering where my heart truly was. It was *through* the act of generous giving that God spoke to me. Without having given to the "wrong" cause, I would not have found the right one.

Recently I had an opportunity to give again. This time I confidently gave an amount to the organization that I really wanted to support. No regrets. Just a joyful gift. And all it cost me was a beautiful mistake.

Don't Do Nothing

Sometimes doing one imperfect but beautiful thing can lead you to more beautiful things later on, if you are listening for God. Contrast that with doing nothing. Most of the time doing nothing leads to more nothing.

It was through the risk (and arguably the "wrong" risk) that I was able to discover the right risk. And I'd rather do that than still have the first gift in my possession, doing nothing, sitting in my checking account.

While there is no end to buyer's remorse, we should ban "giver's regret." Even if we give to someone who doesn't appreciate the gift, it's okay. We still *gave*. Learn from it. Move on.

You're going to make mistakes. Guaranteed.

Just make them beautiful mistakes.

Outcomes Gone Wild

Years ago I was up late, praying. I was desperate to sense more of God in my life. I wanted to hear Him, if He was out there. I told Him I'd do anything—*anything*—that He asked of me, if He would only speak.

I had prayed this prayer many times before. What's weird is that I sensed God speak every time. It's just that every time God spoke, He asked me to do something, well, stupid. So I usually didn't do it.

That night, I sensed God say, "I want you to go down to the 7-Eleven and tell whoever is working there that I love them."

Are You kidding? Are You sure You don't want me to memorize a book of the Bible or something? C'mon, it's like two in the morning. I'm already in my pajamas.

"You don't have to change if you don't want to," God said.

I took that to mean I didn't have to put on jeans over my pajama bottoms. So I put on a robe and slippers, and then I got in my car and drove to the 7-Eleven. Walking into the store, I felt (and looked) like a nut. There were a few people shopping, so I pretended to browse in the candy section. I was determined that my embarrassment should not have a large audience.

After the last customer left the store, I hesitantly walked up to the lady at the cash register. I stammered and finally said, "Uh. I know this sounds strange..."

She was probably reaching for the silent alarm.

"But, uh... I feel like I'm supposed to tell you that God loves you."

The woman looked at me and said, "I know."

I blushed, said "Okay," and left the 7-Eleven.

Years later, that woman won the Nobel Peace Prize and thanked me in her speech.

No she didn't. I never heard from her again.

Sometimes we take risks not because of the outcome we're sure it will produce in others, but because of the outcome it might produce in *us:* namely, becoming the kind of people who are likely to hear God and then go out and risk for His sake. The people who are more likely to make idiots of themselves at 7-Eleven are the ones who will move to Los Angeles to launch the adventure of their lives.

This is the life God is calling us to live. A life of trust. A life of adventure.

There is a huge difference between caring about outcomes and being controlled by outcomes. We can't control what we get out of life; we can control only what we put into it. We can't control the outcomes of our taking risks... We can only control *if we risk.*

At one of the first Spark Groups, a university student named Nathan decided he wanted to compose a song and perform it for a girl who, as far as I could tell, didn't know Nathan existed. (If you think the rest of us weren't eager to show up the following week to hear how things turned out, you've never watched reality television.)

The next week Nathan walked in with a huge smile on his face. He told us how nervous he had been. He had composed a song (it wasn't very good, he said), and then he approached the girl he wanted to sing to.

"So it went well?" we asked.

He laughed. "No!" Then he made a hand gesture like a plane crashing. "Crash and burn," he said. "It freaked her out."

He had failed fantastically.

So all of us raised our metaphorical glasses and toasted. "Mazel tov!" (Literally, "good destiny!") "Salud!" ("To life!")

For Nathan, writing a song and singing it to a girl wasn't only about trying to get a date. It was also about becoming the kind of person who wasn't afraid to love. He was sad, sure. But in the ache he was able to enjoy the thrill of having made a beautiful choice.

One of the most common reasons we don't risk is because we're afraid of the outcome. By definition, that's what a risk is: you engage in an action where the outcome is unknown. Life is wild. It cannot be tamed; it can only be chosen.

So choose something beautiful.

FIFTEEN

On Becoming Strong

//////////

*The value of challenges, obstacles,
and all the other stuff we don't like*

Recently I was on a panel talking about how to turn inspiration into action. Over the past few years I've been in the company of people who are far more talented than I am, and this night was no exception. My fellow panelists were directors of nonprofits, project managers for Pepsi, iPhone game designers, and one fella who oversaw President Obama's social-media campaign when he ran for his first term.

I didn't really belong on the panel, but I enjoyed being there. These people were brilliant and I learned a ton. Yet something kept coming up during the discussion that concerned me. It centered on the idea of "reducing friction."

Friction is used to describe the obstacles standing in the way of a person's taking action. In the recent past, if I wanted to donate money to an organization, I would have to locate my checkbook, write a check, put it in an envelope, address it, find a stamp, and drop it in a mailbox. Today you have to do nothing more than send a text, and the donation amount is added to your phone bill, which you probably pay through an automatic deduction from your checking account.

Stamps, addresses, and envelopes in a world of text donations would be called *friction*. It's what often prevents people from taking action.

On the night of the panel, most of the discussion and questions focused on removing friction as a way to help people move from inaction to action. Considering our audience, that idea makes sense. Most of the people were tech savvy and involved with some form of online commerce. They were trying to figure out ways to make it easier for people to access what they were providing—whether for financial gain or the social good.

Fortunately for everyone in the room, it has never been easier to get people to engage with what you're offering, whether the engagement is media impressions on your Facebook page or people donating to the Red Cross by texting a number on a mobile device.

It has inspired the word *slacktivism,* a hybrid of *slacker* and *activism.* Yet what if, in our attempt to make everything easier, something has gotten lost? What happens to us as individuals and as societies when ease and comfort start becoming operative values?

When we remove friction, things get easier, sure. But something else happens too. We get weaker.

Create a culture where everything is easy, and I'll show you a culture whose days are numbered. We need to remind ourselves that friction can be a good thing. Specifically, friction accomplishes two functions that are essential to our becoming who we long to be: First, friction unearths desire. Second, it cultivates strength.

What Do You Want?

There's a saying about self-leadership that has quickly become one of my favorites: Self-leadership is like doing the high jump. Throw your feet over and your heart will follow.

Often we want our hearts to change *before* we act. But nothing helps the human heart soften faster than choosing to risk. Too often we want God to give us passion so we can act. But in reality it's the other way around. We first begin moving with God, and *then* He begins to soften our hearts.

Motion creates emotion because motion comes up against friction. Have you ever achieved a goal that came too easily, and afterward you didn't appreciate it? Ever had the experience of wanting something very badly, but when you pursued it, you found that it was much harder to obtain than you expected?

Friction forces you to fully explore the question, Do I really want this? It creates a moment in which you have to evaluate what you want, what you care about, what you value. It forces you to dig deep and access a kind of desire that doesn't surface very often.

It has been noted that Jesus, more often than not, seemed to try to talk people *out* of following Him. He would respond to questions with a question. Or He would answer a question by telling an odd story. Or, as happened again and again, He would list all the reasons why a decision to follow Him was a guarantee of hardship and most likely suffering.

Jesus tended to create friction as a way to reveal what people truly wanted. I think this is why Jesus was constantly asking people what it was they wanted, even when the answer seemed obvious. If a blind man comes up to you and asks for mercy, there's a high probability that he wants you to heal his blindness. Yet Jesus still asks, "What do you want?"[1]

Jesus wasn't playing hard to get. He was asking the tough questions as a way to help people move into a healthier future.

I think this also explains why Jesus invited some of those who had requested something from Him to immediately go do some seemingly irrelevant thing. He healed a blind man by covering his eyes with spit-infused mud. After doing that, Jesus told the man to go to a certain place before washing off the mud.[2] To another it was, "Get up, take your mat and go home."[3] It was friction. It's being confronted by the tough questions: Do you really want this? Are you willing to do what it takes to get it, even when the required act seems to have no relation whatever to your getting what you're after?

Strength Training

The second role friction plays is that it develops strength. Friction helps you grow stronger in ways you didn't know were possible.

Every time you exercise you experience the benefits of friction. You stack more plates on the weight machine, creating more friction, to shred the muscle so that it grows back stronger. Your will functions much the same way. You ask God for patience, and suddenly your life becomes more difficult. Has God abandoned you, or is He simply answering your prayer? You ask God for more confidence, and He leads you into places where you are forced to become more confident. You ask God for strength, and He puts a little more weight on the barbell you're lifting.

Jesus's statement to His followers regarding taking His "light yoke" is quoted frequently. A yoke was a farming tool used in first-century agriculture. You would put a yoke on a large animal to till soil or carry large loads. What we don't realize is that this was His way of inviting us to accept more weight for strength training. He said His burden is light and that He is gentle, so people sometimes wrongly assume that it's not a burden at all—that somehow *gentleness* means "effortless." Nothing could be further from the truth.

Read what Paul of Tarsus wrote years later, in line with Jesus's statement:

> No temptation has seized you except what is common to man. And God is faithful; he will not let you be tempted beyond what you can bear. But when you are tempted, he will also provide a way out so that you can stand up under it.[4]

Paul was pointing out that God is a Trainer. Not for our physical bodies but for our character. Not for our arms but for our wills. He won't put so much weight on the bar that it breaks you, but He will definitely put the weight on if you want to grow stronger. And who doesn't want to grow stronger?

Fairy Tales Gone Boring

When I was a kid I loved fairy tales. Thankfully they were immortalized by the wonderful storytellers at Disney in the late eighties and early nineties. The folks who made *Aladdin*, *The Lion King*, and *Beauty and the Beast* ingrained in me the magic of fairy tales and how they reveal our deepest desires about the world we find ourselves in.[5]

If you are a lover of fairy tales, you know already that they abide by certain rules. One example: in fairy tales involving a fairy godmother, she always comes in after everything else has been tried. You won't see her until the main character has exhausted all other options.

Doesn't this seem cruel? I mean, *Where was the stupid godmother all this time?*

Then again, it would be weird if the fairy godmother came in before she was really needed. I mean, can you imagine if she showed up right at the beginning? What would it do to *Cinderella*? Plus, it would make for a *really* short story.

When the mythic journey is inverted, things start to get a little ridiculous. Can you imagine a fairy tale with no struggle?

Dorothy lands in Oz and immediately a wizard appears. The wizard whips up some courage for the lion, a heart for the tin man, and a brain for the scarecrow. Dorothy gets a pair of shoes and a ride in a hot-air balloon, which whisks her straight to Kansas. She wakes up in bed, back home with her family.

There's no place like home? How would Dorothy know? Nothing happened.

Or take Aladdin: he meets a girl, discovers she's the princess, asks her to marry him, she says yes, and they get married. No lamp. No Robin Williams. Fade to black. Roll credits.

What?

It's not just about entertainment. We intuitively know that something important is happening in the journey. We know that while Dorothy is looking for the wizard, while Aladdin is trying to win the heart of the princess, when Belle is trying to get away from the beast, something else is happening. Dorothy is discovering something about herself. She's being refined. Aladdin is becoming the kind of person who will someday be a king. The beast's heart is softening. Belle is learning to see deeper than first impressions allow. Often that something else is just as important, if not more important, than the question of whether the lead character will achieve his or her goal before the credits roll.

We know this to be true of stories on-screen and in books. Yet when it comes to our own lives, we want it to be different. I admit that I'd prefer journey-less faith. I want instant progress. I want fast-acting relief rather than slow-moving relationship. I don't want to be transformed slowly through struggle and opposition; I want to feel better *now*.

And yet if God magically snapped His fingers to fix my life, something would be...missing. It's almost like I'd be missing the entire point. Something is supposed to be happening, something sacred, while you and I are on the journey.

It's not just about the information. It's not even primarily about the risk. With Spark Groups we call people to take risks, sure. Some of the experiments turn out well; some don't. Some are more meaningful than others. But the risks themselves aren't even the point.

Something else is going on.

What Happens While It's Happening

We call Spark Groups "applied learning environments." The purpose of these groups is not to give people a chance to get together and talk about taking four risks that hopefully will impact their lives. There's nothing wrong with that, but there's something else happening that is far more exciting.

The purpose is to invite people into a deeper engagement with their own lives. This is something that lasts longer than any choice you might make during the five-week experience. When people take risks together, they develop a certain kind of worldview, one where people lean into life rather than away from it. One where people begin thinking creatively and compassionately about themselves and the world around them.

The most cherished stories that have come out of Spark Groups are from people whose group took place a long time ago. Occasionally we'll get e-mails or hear stories from folks explaining how being a part of the group didn't simply help them take a few risks over the course of five weeks, but the experience helped them develop a value for risk that now filters into everything they do. It helped them engage life at a deeper level. The message of healthy risk-taking and self-challenge became a way of life rather than simply a glimpse of life.

It wasn't a lecture or book or class. It wasn't necessarily taking four risks or spending time with a certain group of people. It was all of those things, combined, to create a culture that shaped the way they saw the world. For five weeks they were a part of a culture that valued healthy risk-taking and self-challenge.

On Cultivating Appetites

When I was a kid, I hated tomatoes. I loved ketchup, but I hated tomatoes. We had a garden in our backyard, and my parents always looked forward to tomato season. I thought my parents were nuts.

And then something changed. Maybe my mom snuck a tomato onto something without my noticing, and I bit into it. The huge burger had a little something extra, something nice and cool. What was it?

Tomato.

Last Thanksgiving I was thinking about this as I was tossing cherry tomatoes in my mouth as a snack. *I love these things,* I thought.

There are days when I crave tomatoes. If I eat a burger without tomatoes, something doesn't seem right. I look forward to those healthy little mixed vegetable dishes because I know they'll have tomatoes.

What happened is this: I cultivated an appetite for it.

Tomatoes aren't the only thing we can cultivate an appetite for. Anything that's an acquired taste—from coffee to licorice—at first tastes a little gross. But after a while you get used to it. And if you're not careful, you'll begin to have an addiction to it.

Good works the same way. Good is like tomatoes, like coffee. It's an acquired taste. You have to cultivate an appetite for it. You do this by being exposed to it.

This is one of the biggest goals of Spark Groups. Through taking healthy risks that make you a better person or the world a better place, you begin to develop a deeper appetite for good. At first it might not be very tasty. Taking even a small risk can be more difficult than it sounds. And that is why we have to practice. We have to develop the skill of challenging ourselves.

The Art of Self-Challenge

We want the act of making healthy choices to become a natural and authentic part of who we are. But before something can become a habit, it often is a hassle. Put another way: if we want new habits to become instinctual, then they must first be intentional. And in order for that to happen, we have to practice the sacred art of self-challenge.

I don't want to freak you out, but what we're really talking about is obedience. Obedience to God is the path that leads to Life. It's the path that transforms you into the person you long to be.

And obedience always requires risk.

What's amazing is that much of our obedience is instinctual. In at least some areas of life, we naturally make healthy choices. We naturally smile at a stranger, or perhaps we have a great work ethic or are naturally curious or easygoing.

Yet we can't define obedience solely in terms of what comes naturally. Often our greatest moments of obedience come when it is least natural. Perhaps our natural tendency in certain situations is unhealthy or hurtful. Or perhaps what we naturally want to do is *nothing*, to avoid taking action when action is called for. In these moments we have to choose something else, something we don't want to do, something that, most likely, will move us into the space of the unknown.

I want to be a person who is able to act—who is able to obey—even when it's unnatural.

Intentionality and risk are the ways we develop a greater capacity to obey. When we say, "I'm going to do this thing that I wouldn't normally do," we are developing the capacity to grow into the people we were meant to be.

When Jesus invited people to follow Him, He was inviting them to obey Him. There are parts of you that already reflect God's character, parts of your uniqueness that are expressions of something God wanted to say when He created you. Those are already consistent with following Jesus.

Maybe it's your smile.

Maybe it's your way with people.

Maybe it's your work ethic.

Maybe it's your sense of right and wrong.

Maybe it's your intelligence or your curiosity for life.

Maybe it's your sense of responsibility or your flare for fun.

These things are good just the way they are. It's easy to obey when God calls us to things we naturally love. When God calls us to the stuff we already like (which happens a lot more than we realize), it's one of the great pleasures of life.

Yet there is much about you and me that comes naturally but *doesn't* honor God. In those areas we need to devote an unnatural amount of energy to develop ourselves far beyond what we're good at. This doesn't mean we do what we're not good at just for the sake of doing something we dislike. It means that we dive into the outer limits of what we're naturally good at, which usually involves developing un- natural skills such as perseverance, fortitude, and patience.

These are the best moments for practicing what I call the art of self- challenge. It's when you challenge yourself for the purpose of devel- oping your capacity to be comfortable doing what's uncomfortable. This isn't masochistic; it's not pain for the sake of pain. It's intention- ally pursuing the unnatural side of Good.

Personal progress hinges on your ability to challenge yourself. Shy away from challenge and you'll create a frictionless world for your- self. Your will begins to atrophy, and your life, even if it appears to be going well, will not be able to stand up under much pressure.

Yet when you lean into challenge, when you cultivate an appetite for healthy risk-taking, you begin to flex your will and to experience life in a new way.

For example, not exercising comes naturally to me. I'm one of the best nonexercisers in Southern California. I could teach graduate courses on "Doing Only What Feels Good," and I'd easily ace a PhD program in Applied Procrastination. I am professionally equipped to not do any exercise.

When I first moved to Los Angeles, I ate Lunchables like they were a food group. I didn't know how to take better care of myself. (Or maybe I didn't want to.)

But there came a time when I got tired of being tired. I wanted better posture, to be more useful on moving days, and to feel like I was being a better steward of the only body God gave me.

So I did what was unnatural. I went out and ran ten miles.

The next day I couldn't walk, and I think that week I got sick because my immune system more or less freaked out. I didn't run again for ten months.

About a year later I decided to approach my physical health differently. I decided to start going on walks. For the first week, they were ten-minute walks. Then I decided to go on jogs. Ten-minute jogs. Then twenty-minute jogs. I told myself if I could go jogging every day for three months, that I'd get a gym membership.

Three months later I walked into a gym of my own volition for the very first time. My brother-in-law sells health products to supplement exercise, and he gave me some for free. Six months later, I was working out three times a week and drinking health shakes. All I was missing was a yoga mat and a Toyota Prius.

One of my favorite recent Sparks came from an actor friend. She came to a Spark Group in downtown Los Angeles with a bunch of my friends. We caught up during the week, and she told me that her risk was to intentionally put herself in a more positive and spiritually potent environment.

Translation: she was going to go to church for the first time.

This may not seem like a big risk for many of you, but for her it was huge. She grew up going to a strict Episcopalian school and because of that—and a lot of other reasons—church wasn't a space she felt comfortable in.

Yet she wanted to challenge herself in a positive way. She wanted to take at least one risk in a direction that might be beneficial spiritually. She had met some folks at Mosaic, and they seemed "normal," or at least crazy in the same ways she was. So she decided to check it out.

In that moment there were two beautiful things happening. She was putting herself in a positive space, and she was becoming the kind of person who was not afraid to pursue beautiful things.

Later she told me how just hanging out at the Spark Group for one night began changing the way she saw her life. "I started looking at challenges as opportunities," she said. "Instead of leaning away from situations, I started leaning toward them."

When you step out into risk, it's not simply about the risk you are taking. Yes, you will make beautiful choices that make you a better person and the world a better place. But just as important, you will intentionally create friction in your life. This friction will unearth your desire, letting you know what you really want. It will, in the end, make you stronger. It will help you reach down to excavate the goodness that God has placed inside you.

And you will have taken one small step toward changing your world.

SIXTEEN

How to Spark Your World

//////////

*Receiving the gift God
most longs to give you*

There are generally two types of gifts.

The first is when you receive something you want—the latest gadget or a stylish dress in a store's display window. Your friend notices you are drawn to a certain thing, then goes and purchases it for you. Pretty simple. The gift is about you and what you want.

The other type of gift is just as meaningful (if not more so), but it differs slightly. These are gifts through which people share a piece of who they are with you. This is when someone shows you his favorite movie or takes you to her favorite restaurant. These gifts are less about you as an individual and more about the relationship.

Receiving the second type of gift presents a wonderful opportunity to learn about someone else. If a friend takes you to his favorite restaurant, the point of the evening is not merely to enjoy good food on someone else's dime. The bigger purpose is to learn more about the other person. The point is to receive not just the gift of a great meal, but also to receive *the person* in a small way.

Over the past few years, I've really grown to value this second perspective on gift giving. I've learned to appreciate gifts not when they're totally about me, but when they are also a reflection of the giver. When a gift reveals something beautiful about the person giving it, the exchange becomes a unique act of friendship and love. When we love something, we want to share it with others, especially others we love. I love seeing movies with people, even if I've already seen the movie, because I love sharing the experience.

I used to invite friends over for *The Usual Suspects* parties just so I could enjoy having them experience what is, in my opinion, the best ending to a movie *ever*. We naturally share what we love. We naturally invite others into what we love.

I think God is the same way.

God's Favorite Gift

As the story goes in the scriptures, an angel appeared to a thirteen-year-old girl and told her that God had found favor with her. In other words, God had decided to give her a present.

My older sister was a young girl once. I remember quite viscerally that if you tell a thirteen-year-old girl that you're going to give her a present, her response runs along the lines of giddy-loss-of-control elation. It involves yelling and jumping and screaming in a way that threatens to shatter mirrors. And, if you're going to get a thirteen-year-old girl a present, it should be something like a cell phone or an article of clothing or tickets to a Justin Bieber concert.

So you can imagine how this girl felt long ago when an *angel* (I imagine sounding something like a game-show host) said, "You have found favor with God. And what's more, God is going to give you a present!"[1]

Is it a Caboodles case for her makeup? No. A car? Keep dreaming.

No, the angel says. God loves you so much that He's going to make you *pregnant*.

I imagine Mary thinking, *Huh?*

You see, God's favorite gift to give people is the opportunity to serve others. God's favorite blessing, the thing He can't wait to give us, is the opportunity to serve someone else. Because when we engage in the adventure of servanthood, we get a glimpse of what it means to be like God.

This is the movement of God. A movement of servants who are alive and empowered and partnering with God to pull off the impossible and to have a ball doing it.

Every movement is guided by values. For the civil rights movement, it was racial equality. For the Revolutionary War, it was freedom and justice for all. So what are the values of the movement of God? And what does it look like for you and me to become part of the adventure of bringing healing and hope to the world?

Hear the Theme

Every film score has a section known as the theme. It's the melody that anchors the film. When you recall a movie you particularly enjoyed, the theme from the score often comes to mind. (It's the series of notes that recur in varying keys and styles throughout the film.)

Even if you're not paying attention to the music, you'll often leave the theater whistling the theme on your way to the car.

John Williams is one of the most successful theme composers ever. He composed the themes to the Olympics, to NBC's *Nightly News,* and even *Meet the Press.* He wrote the classic, two-note cello theme to *Jaws.* He also composed the scores to the *Star Wars* saga, the Indiana Jones series, *Superman, Schindler's List, Close Encounters of the Third Kind,* the first three of the Harry Potter series, *Jurassic Park, Home Alone, JFK, Hook,* and *E.T.: The Extra-Terrestrial,* just to name a few.

Williams is a genius. He knows how to create a narrative with music that unites the story and becomes an emotional center for listeners to keep coming back to. And just as you find themes in John Williams's music, you can find themes in the pages of the scriptures.

For example, if you read the letters that Paul of Tarsus wrote to first-century communities that were experimenting with the teachings of Jesus, you'll see three themes emerge. In the same way that the *Star Wars* theme weaves in and out of all six of George Lucas's films, so do three themes begin to emerge from Paul's writings and life. They are

- **faith,**
- **love,** and
- **hope.**

Like three bullet holes in the corpse of mediocrity. Like the first three drops of rain in the increasingly dry landscape of human relationships.

When you read Paul's writings, you start to feel like he was obsessed with just three things. No matter where he was trying to go with an idea, he ended up with faith, love, and hope. For Caesar, all roads led to Rome. For Paul, all his letters led to three ideas. You see them in 1 Corinthians 13. Twice in 1 Thessalonians. Once in Colossians. These three ideas are what he sensed were the themes to what it means to be fully alive—to be connected in a life-giving way to God.

Faith, love, and hope are crucial to what it means to create a healthy life, yet I almost hesitate to even mention them. They are beautiful, yet dangerous, ideas. They are so familiar to those who have read the scriptures that they can easily be neutered through overuse.

Much of my spiritual journey over the last fifteen years has involved unlearning what I was taught growing up. The unlearning process involves using different words that capture, in a fresh way, the essence of ancient ideas. New words for old truth can inspire you to action.

So for faith, love, and hope, I have adopted the words *risk, compassion,* and *optimism.* Words shape culture and individual lives, so I'd like to walk you through the ways these three words unleash the initial power of faith, love, and hope.

Risk (Where Faith Meets Life)

Risk is the central narrative of the scriptures. When I do Spark Group trainings with faith communities, I always have participants do this exercise:

1. Pick any person in the scriptures that comes to mind.
2. Identify the risk God called that person to take.

This is surprisingly easy. And once people get going, it's hard to get them to stop. Abraham: stopped living with his parents at age seventy and moved into no man's land to start his own nation. Moses: even with a speech impediment, he stood up to the most powerful man in the world to liberate an enslaved people. Mary: endured the shame of people assuming she had been unfaithful to her fiancé. Joseph: remained committed to a teenage girl, his fiancée, who in the eyes of their neighbors and extended family was almost certainly an adulteress.

Samson.

Ruth.

The apostle Paul.

Rahab.

The twelve fellas who quit their jobs to follow Jesus, most of whom were later killed for doing so.

The people whose stories are recorded in the history of the scriptures all took risks—often huge risks—to be a part of what God was doing in the world. It seems like a prerequisite for being mentioned in the narrative of the movement of God is the willingness and courage to risk.

Like God's people throughout history, we can jump into life in ways that *only we can* so that God can move in ways *we cannot*. Call it faith if you want, but in terms of everyday life, it's *risk*. And it's through risk that God can change our lives.

For Steven Ma, who participated in a Spark Group several years ago, it started with a risk to pursue something he'd loved all his life: graphic design.

"I was in a really depressing season of my life where I was unemployed," Steven said. "I knew I wanted to do something significant, but nothing was really coming to mind. I felt like I had all these skills and potential, but no opportunities were coming my way. So I just kind of sat around waiting for something to happen."

He was invited by a friend to join a Spark Group in Whittier, California. "The whole idea of taking small risks to accomplish a goal really appealed to me," Steven said. For the first few weeks he took what he now calls "random risks," such as exercising more and being more intentional about connecting with friends. "But then one week I decided to take a risk to develop my creative side more. I decided to revisit a talent I loved when I was younger—graphic design." He redesigned his web page and then replied to several Craigslist postings to see if he could earn money using his design talent.

One of the people who had posted an ad on Craigslist responded to Steven's inquiry. He needed design help related to an iPhone app he was creating. Steven had exactly the skills that were needed.

Those first few risks changed Steven's life forever. A year later his dream evolved from freelance work to running his own graphic-design company: Spark Up Arts (Sparkuparts.com). Steven Ma took a risk, and it unlocked potential and opportunity. He got off unemployment and launched a new career that exceeded anything he had imagined.

But it didn't stop there.

"After creating my own design company, I began exploring some other dreams that I had kind of pushed aside," he continued. For most of his life, Steven had been interested in Africa and had wanted to do something that would serve that continent. So his next risk was to tell other people that he wanted to start a for-profit company that would equip and empower a group of people in that part of the world.

"Going off the confidence I had gained from starting a smaller business, I thought, *Okay, it's really not that hard. Now I can build off that and take it even further.* Participating in a Spark Group helped me really understand that you don't have to create a company in a day, that your dreams are really just the culmination of a series of smaller risks."

That summer Steven went to Kenya, an international journey that had started with a small risk to start a design company. His dream to help serve others was becoming reality. His risks evolved from getting a job for himself to creating jobs for others.

This is how the movement of God works. Our risks cease to become merely about ourselves—they begin to extend to our community and the world.

We risk so others can thrive.

We risk so God can love.

Compassion (The Gritty Word for Love)

This leads to our second value: compassion. It's not just *any* risk that is important. After all, people take stupid risks all the time. Just think about Bernie Madoff and Johnny Knoxville. Cheating people in a crooked investment scam (Madoff) and filming yourself in the act of squeezing lemons over your own paper cuts (Knoxville) are not a wise, or beneficial, investment of one's time or creativity. Some risks are just immoral, some are supremely stupid, and in either case they are (thankfully) not what God is calling us toward.

In chapter 8 we looked at a different meaning of *passion*, which is linked closely to suffering. It shouldn't surprise us when we discover that the word *compassion* means "to suffer *with*." Too often we define compassion as a sympathetic feeling. "I feel so sorry for that homeless person." But compassion isn't sympathy. It isn't even empathy—where you feel what the other person is feeling. No, compassion has less to do with your feelings and more to do with your *actions.*

Compassion is risk lived out in community. It is the force that drives us to live our most extraordinary lives.

Steven Ma knew he would never be able to start a company on his own that would reach around the globe to Kenya. So he sent an e-mail to twenty friends asking for any help they could provide. Most people didn't know how they could help, but they were willing to do what was needed. That e-mail snowballed into a series of meetings with friends and with friends of friends—almost all of whom shared their expertise with Steven.

He summed it up this way: "Over and over again I would just ask people, 'So what should my next step be?' and they would help me take the next small risk in the right direction."

Through this informal community of friends, Steven began moving forward toward what would become the company Intrinsic, whose mission is to help communities in Africa rise above poverty through sustainable business (Intrinsicstyles.com). Today, Intrinsic partners with artists in Africa, utilizing their own skills, talents, and resources to help them design lifestyle accessories.

Steven was motivated to create a company in Kenya because he cared. Over the years, as he became more connected with the people of Kenya, his love for the people grew. Now he finds his own success in the success of his Kenyan friends. In partnering to unleash the potential of others, he finds that his own potential is unleashed.

Achieving our potential isn't meant to be some narcissistic venture into ourselves for our own benefit. We must be driven to greatness because that is what is needed to help a desperate world.

Love is the only force that can fuel the life we were created to live. No amount of guilt or shame can produce the same results. It's love that enables parents to accomplish the superhuman feats necessary to raise children. And love is what enables all of us to go beyond ourselves in taking the risk to change the world.

On the whiteboard in front of my computer are the words "Write with compassion." Before I speak publicly, reminding myself of the worth of my audience is the only thing that calms me. There are people in the audience with real hopes and fears, and I have an opportunity to say something that might lead them to live more deeply—to find Life.

My best moments are always moments of compassion. Compassion can fill your soul when you're hurting. *Love* (the tried-and-true word) empowers us and makes us strong when we feel weak.

Love and compassion always expand out toward others. They extend beyond your own life. So whom are you serving? Whom do you love? What would it look like if you were to begin connecting with people who could use your help? After all, everyone needs a little help.

Optimism (The Energy That Sustains Risk)

The third value is optimism, which is central to an odd contradiction. It is possible to live a life of compassion and risk and still be consumed by a sense of despair and loss. This has been called the "angry activist complex." These are the people who take extraordinary risks and give deeply of themselves, yet in the end they burn out. They become angry when other people don't join the cause, which leads to feelings of frustration and helplessness.

These people risked much but then lost hope. Their view of the present as well as the future is bleak. You can't maintain the courage that is necessary to risk in love (compassion) if all you have is the willingness to put yourself out there for a worthy cause. There has to be some energy underneath it that can sustain a life of giving. That energy is *hope*—or in our terminology, *optimism.*

Every human needs to believe that tomorrow can be better than today. Hope is the idea that the potential for progress and positive change is real, not just rooted in naive idealism. The injustice of inequality motivated Dr. Martin Luther King Jr. to act. But it was his dream for the future that kept him acting.

I heard someone say that relationships die the moment one person stops believing that the other person can grow. Relationships and communities alike die when we give up hope.

The irony of hope is that it is oriented toward the future but can be chosen in the present. When we take risks of compassion, we find ourselves growing. We can look back and say, "Look how far we've come!" We can become less selfish, less greedy. We can become better listeners, more forgiving, less controlling. We can progress.

When we choose to grow in the present, we kindle optimism for the future.

When I first moved to Los Angeles, I spent a lot of time investing in junior high school students—most of whom lived in pretty rough parts of town. One of our volunteers lived at one of the most expensive houses in Pasadena, the house that was used as Dr. Emmett Brown's house in the *Back to the Future* trilogy. (This makes this particular house the coolest house in the history of humankind.)

If that weren't enough, this house also is a billion-dollar museum with million-dollar furniture. As a grad student, my friend got to live in the servants' quarters.

So I thought, *What better place to have a junior high retreat?* Somehow I convinced my friend to let our group of students hold a retreat there, which meant we had dozens of thirteen-year-olds running around in a billion-dollar museum.

One of the students was a kid named Bobby. He was also one of the rowdiest kids in the group. He had little respect for authority (or at least little respect for me) and was nearly impossible to control.

Whenever we held retreats, we had a Three Strike policy: if you broke the rules three times, you were sent home. About thirty minutes into the event, Bobby had received two strikes. We still had eighteen hours to go and things were not looking good.

I sat Bobby down on the couch and asked, "Do you *want* to go home!"

He looked at me with tears in his eyes. "No."

I said, "I don't want you to go home either. You've got one strike left. Do you think you can make it?"

In a moment of great honesty, Bobby said, "I don't think I can."

I sat next to him and asked, "Well, are you willing to at least try?"

He thought about it, and with a sniffle that only a thirteen-year-old boy can make, he looked up and said, "Yeah."

That night was the longest night of my life. We did everything we could to match our patience to the level of Bobby's effort. He'd start to say something mean or do something destructive and one of our leaders would say, "Bobby!" and he'd stop and give a huge sigh and move on to something else. Eighteen hours later, when the parents came to pick up their kids, Bobby had 2.99 strikes.

When his mother showed up, he looked at me and yelled, "I made it!"

After all the parents left with their kids, the volunteers collapsed on the expensive furniture and said, "*We* made it!"

Sometimes people need just a little bit of hope. They need to have someone believe that their lives can be better tomorrow than they are today. That *they* can be better tomorrow than they were today. And

Chapter 2

1. TED is a nonprofit devoted to Ideas Worth Spreading. It began in 1984 as a conference bringing together people from three worlds: Technology, Entertainment, Design. TED now holds two annual conferences—the TED Conference in Long Beach and Palm Springs each spring, as well as the TEDGlobal conference in Edinburgh, UK, each summer. www.ted.com/pages/about.

2. Elizabeth Gilbert, "Nurturing Creativity" (speech, TED conference, Monterey, CA, February 2009), www.ted.com/talks/elizabeth_gilbert_on_genius.html/.

3. Gilbert, "Nurturing Creativity."

4. Gilbert, "Nurturing Creativity."

5. See Galatians 5:22–23.

6. For a deeper conversation on these intrinsic longings, I strongly recommend Erwin McManus's book *Soul Cravings* (Nashville, TN: Thomas Nelson, 2006).

7. John 10:10, author's paraphrase.

8. For more information about Mission Year, check out www.mission year.org.

9. John 4:13–14, author's paraphrase.

Chapter 3

1. Jason Jaggard, "Giants Sleeping."

2. See Matthew 25:14–30.

3. Bob Goff, interview by Ken Coleman, One Question, http://ken coleman.podbean.com/feed/.

Chapter 4

1. This ancient story (see Genesis 11:1–9) is still relevant today, reflecting the major realities of our lives.

2. Genesis 11:6, author's paraphrase.

3. Marianne Williamson, *A Return to Love* (New York: HarperCollins, 1992), 190.

4. Erwin McManus shaped my thinking on character through his book *Uprising: A Revolution of the Soul* (Nashville, TN: Thomas Nelson, 2006).

5. See Philippians 2:8 (Christ humbled Himself); Philippians 2:7 (Christ became a Servant); Mark 9:35 (Jesus said, "If anyone wants to be first, he must be the very last, and the servant of all"); and finally, Matthew 20:28 (Jesus "did not come [to earth] to be served, but to serve, and to give his life as a ransom for many").

Chapter 5

1. See Strengthsfinder.com.

2. See Matthew 11:19.

3. For more on this phenomenon, see Charles G. Costello, "A Critical Review of Seligman's Laboratory Experiments on Learned Helplessness and Depression in Humans," *Journal of Abnormal Psychology*, 87, no. 1 (1978): 49–74.

4. For more on this, see Greg L. Hawkins and Cally Parkinson, *Reveal: Where Are You?* (South Barrington, IL: Willow Creek Association, 2007).

Chapter 6

1. Marcus Buckingham and Donald O. Clifton, *Now, Discover Your Strengths* (New York: Free Press, 2001), 29.

2. George Bernard Shaw, *Back to Methuselah*, Act 1, www.online-literature.com/george_bernard_shaw/back-to-methuselah/2/.

3. Dialogue from *The Blind Side,* screenplay by John Lee Hancock and Michael Lewis, directed by John Lee Hancock (Alcon Entertainment, 2009), www.imdb.com/title/tt0878804/quotes.

Chapter 7

1. For the full story, see Luke 11:24–26.
2. Erwin McManus exposed me to the insights of this passage when he spoke at the Willow Creek Leadership Summit in 2003.
3. See Matthew 25:14–30, especially verses 24–29.
4. See Steve Saccone, *Protégé* (Westmont, IL: IVP Books, 2012).

Chapter 8

1. Joshua Davis, "The Perfect Human," *Wired,* no. 15.01, January 2007, www.wired.com/wired/archive/15.01/ultraman.html.
2. See Ephesians 4:26.
3. 1 Thessalonians 4:3.
4. 1 Thessalonians 4:3 (NLT).
5. Philippians 4:8 (ESV).
6. Dean Karnazes, quoted in Joshua Davis, "The Perfect Human," *Wired,* no. 15.01, January 2007, www.wired.com/wired/archive /15.01/ultraman.html. Additional information taken from TheRelay.com.

Chapter 9

1. Though verified elsewhere, I learned this from the brilliant lectures of Dan Tocchini, www.dantocchini.com.
2. This is a modification from Andy Clark's book *Natural-Born Cyborgs* (New York: Oxford University Press, 2003).
3. Anais Nin, "Anais Nin Quotes," Thinkexist.com, http://thinkexist .com/quotation/we_don-t_see_things_as_they_are-we_see _them_as_we/146971.html.

Chapter 10

1. See Genesis 12:1–6.

Chapter 11

1. Found at www.ideafinder.com.

Chapter 12

1. John 5:17; John 5:19.
2. See John 3:3–8; to read the entire conversation between Jesus and Nicodemus, see John 3:1–21.
3. See James 2:20; 2:15–18.
4. See James 2:21–24; 2:26.
5. Dialogue from *Ocean's Eleven*, screenplay by Ted Griffin, directed by Steven Soderberg (Warner Bros., 2001), www.moviefanatic .com/quotes/youre-either-in-or-youre-out-right-now-what- is-it-its-a-plane-ti/.
6. To read the entire conversation between Jesus and Nicodemus, and to check on its similarity to a scene in *Ocean's Eleven*, see John 3:1–21.

Chapter 13

1. Dialogue from *Ocean's Twelve*, screenplay by George Nolfi, directed by Steven Soderbergh (Warner Bros., 2004), www.subzin.com/quotes/Ocean%27s+Twelve/We+go +into+some+place,+and+all+I+can+do+is+see+the +angles.

Chapter 14

1. www.imdb.com/name/nm0000632/bio.
2. For the whole story, see Matthew 1:18–25.
3. Matthew 1:19.

Chapter 15

1. Matthew 20:32 (ESV).
2. See John 9:6–7.
3. Matthew 9:6.
4. 1 Corinthians 10:13.
5. For more on the magic of fairy tales, see G. K. Chesterton, *Orthodoxy: The Classic Account of a Remarkable Christian Experience* (Colorado Springs, CO: WaterBrook, 1994, 2001), 61–92. Of particular interest is the chapter titled "The Ethics of Elfland."

Chapter 16

1. See Luke 1:30–31.
2. See John 14:12.
3. See Matthew 28:18–20.